T0383536

Internet of Things Security

Internet of Things Security

Principles, Applications, Attacks, and Countermeasures

B. B. Gupta

Megha Quamara

CRC Press
Taylor & Francis Group
Boca Raton London New York

CRC Press is an imprint of the
Taylor & Francis Group, an **informa** business

CRC Press
Taylor & Francis Group
6000 Broken Sound Parkway NW, Suite 300
Boca Raton, FL 33487-2742

Printed on acid-free paper

International Standard Book Number-13: 978-0-367-37396-2 (Hardback)

Visit the Taylor & Francis Web site at
http://www.taylorandfrancis.com

and the CRC Press Web site at
http://www.crcpress.com

Dedicated to my parents and family for their constant support during the course of this book

B. B. Gupta

Dedicated to my mentor, my parents, and my friends for their constant encouragement and belief during the course of this book

Megha Quamara

Contents

List of figures

List of tables

Preface

The Internet of Things (IoT) is defined as an idea of inter-connected devices around us that are capable of sharing information and resources among each other to work for the achievement of a specific goal. It involves devices and technologies with heterogeneous capabilities and properties for the improvement of the efficiency of the resulting applications and to raise economic and social benefits for people. With the growing edge of the concept of the IoT, it becomes necessary to understand and counter the challenges, including security issues, associated with the field. The overall purpose of producing this book is to develop an understanding of the core concepts of the IoT among the readers including architects, developers, researchers, and industrialists in the field so that they can contribute toward its overall development, while at the same time, considering the novel and challenging aspects associated with its adoption. The subject matter of the book explores, and aims at drawing the attention of the reader toward, the existing literature, ongoing research, and possible future research directions in the field.

Specifically, the chapters contained in this book are summarized as follows:

Chapter 1 introduces the concept of the IoT with some related definitions and comprises the events associated with the evolution of the IoT, related statistics, and industrial forecasts provided by well known organizations across the world.

Chapter 2 discusses the architectural model of the IoT in detail, encompassing different layers with a description of the various entities involved, their functionalities, along with security aspects. Moreover, it discusses potential and innovative business models for the IoT including the underlying components, challenges, and technological perspectives.

Chapter 3 discusses various protocols for IoT networks, along with different communication standards, regulation, tools, and datasets for IoT development.

Chapter 4 discusses the challenges associated with the architecture, different entities, underlying technologies, characteristics, and developmental practices in the IoT ecosystem.

Chapter 5 addresses the problem of data explosion in the IoT.

Chapter 6 presents autonomous driving vehicles as an application area of the IoT and highlights the computing paradigms and security issues associated with them.

Acknowledgments

Many people have contributed greatly to this book on the *Internet of Things Security: Principles, Applications, Attacks, and Countermeasures*. The authors would like to acknowledge all of them for their valuable help and generous ideas in improving the quality of this book. With our feelings of gratitude, we would like to introduce them in turn. The first mention is the staff of both CRC Press and Taylor & Francis Group for their constant encouragement, continuous assistance, and untiring support. Without their technical support, this book would not be completed. The next mention is the authors' families for being the source of continuous love, unconditional support, and prayers not only for this work, but throughout our lives. Last, but far from least, we express our heartfelt thanks to the Almighty for bestowing over us the courage to face the complexities of life and complete this work.

B. B. Gupta
Megha Quamara

Authors

B. B. Gupta received a PhD degree from the Indian Institute of Technology, Roorkee, India, in the area of information and cyber security. He has published more than 200 research papers in international journals and conferences of high repute including IEEE, Elsevier, ACM, Springer, Wiley, Taylor & Francis Group, Inderscience, etc. He has visited several countries, i.e., Canada, Japan, the United States, the United Kingdom, Malaysia, Australia, Thailand, China, Hong Kong, Italy, Spain, etc. to present his research work. His biography was selected and published in the 30th Edition of *Marquis Who's Who in the World, 2012*. Dr. Gupta also received the Young Faculty Research Fellowship award from the Ministry of Electronics and Information Technology, Government of India in 2018. He is also working as a principal investigator of various research and development projects. He is serving as an associate editor of IEEE Access, IEEE TII, and the executive editor of IJITCA, Inderscience, respectively. At present, Dr. Gupta is working as an assistant professor in the Department of Computer Engineering, National Institute of Technology, Kurukshetra, India. His research interests include information security, cyber security, mobile security, cloud computing, web security, intrusion detection, and phishing.

Megha Quamara received her master of technology (M.Tech) degree in cyber security from the National Institute of Technology (NIT), Kurukshetra, India, in 2018. She was awarded the Gold Medal for being the best graduating student throughout the course. She received her bachelor of technology (B.Tech) degree in computer science and engineering from the University Institute of Engineering and Technology (UIET), Kurukshetra University, India, in the year 2015, with a First Division with Honour. Her research interests include security in the Internet of Things (IoT) and cloud computing, authentication in smart card technology, security in autonomous vehicles, and data privacy. She has published and presented 11 research papers (including one book chapter) in international platforms of high repute, including Wiley, Elsevier, IEEE, and Springer. She is a co-author of the book *Smart Card Security: Applications, Attacks,* *and Countermeasures* published by CRC Press. She is also serving as a reviewer of various journals and conferences. Soon, she will start pursuing a doctoral program at CEA, Paris, in collaboration with the University of Toulouse, France, where her main area of work will be the safety and security of cyber-physical systems.

Internet of Things – Evolution, Statistics, and Forecasts

1

1.1 INTRODUCTION

The Internet of Things is the idea of seamless integration of physical devices with the Internet that are equipped with sensors, processors, and communication components facilitating sensing, computing, and communication capabilities for perceiving, processing, and exchanging information through the Internet with limited or no human intervention. These devices may include security systems, vehicles, home appliances, electronic gadgets, people, animals, and so forth. User interface is provided for their installation and for providing commands to these devices to control their functionality [1–4]. These devices share data with one another, or they are sent to the local processing units or remote cloud servers for processing.

From its very beginning, the idea of the IoT is transforming various aspects of our everyday lives and has proven to be a revolutionary technological and networking paradigm. Various industries are adopting the concept of the IoT in order to function in a smooth and more efficient manner, with a better understanding of how to deliver enhanced services to the customers and for improving the decision-making process to increase the overall revenue. It encourages business organizations to integrate and adapt new business models, and to monitor the overall business processes for the improvement of business strategies. Network and communication protocols used in IoT networks are highly dependent on the nature of underlying applications. These real-world applications range from consumer-oriented applications, such as smart homes, wearables, and healthcare, to enterprise applications, such as smart cities, agriculture, smart industries, and traffic management. It is not incorrect to say that the current hype of the IoT is immense, and newer IoT-enabled products are coming to the market every day [5–8].

Despite various benefits of the idea of inter-connecting things, the IoT accompanies various challenges as well. Ever-growing Internet-connected devices and data points expand the attack surface that makes security and privacy aspects that are often ignored crucial. Beyond this, setting up infrastructure capabilities involving large numbers of devices that are of a heterogeneous nature is another challenging aspect. Many of the IoT-enabled initiatives have failed due to lack of effective integration and collaboration among various components, while at the same time creating a new culture of the technology. Even with the availability of resources, poor analysis and decision-making prevent industries from obtaining substantial benefits from the IoT. It is thus worth digging into knowing what the IoT exactly is and how its different components are inter-related.

The next section presents some of the definitions presented by well-known organizations from around the globe to understand the concept of the IoT. In later sections, evolutionary aspects of the IoT along with industrial statistics and forecasts are discussed.

1.2 DEFINITION OF IoT

National Institute of Standards and Technology defines the IoT as a system involving sensing, actuation, communication, and computation components [9,10]. IoT devices are different from the conventional digital devices in the sense that these can interact with the physical world, cannot be accessed, monitored, and managed through conventional means, and are characterized by enhanced security and privacy capabilities in terms of availability, effectiveness, and efficiency. According to Gartner, the IoT is the network consisting of physical objects having embedded technology for communication and sensing and for interaction with internal states and the external environment [11]. It will have a great economic impact through the transformation of traditional enterprises into digital and smart businesses. It will also facilitate new business models that would improve the efficiency and employee-customer engagement.

Recommendation ITU-T Y.2060 defines the IoT as a global infrastructure for the information society, which enables advanced and high-end services through inter-connection of physical and virtual things based on existing and progressing information and communication technologies that support inter-operability [12]. Physical things are a part of the physical world, and these can be sensed, actuated, and connected. These can interact with each other via gateway, without gateway, or directly. On the other hand, virtual things (e.g., application software, multi-media content) are a part of the information world, and these can be stored, processed, and accessed remotely. Fundamental characteristics of the IoT include inter-connectivity, heterogeneity, dynamic state changes, and scalability.

Cisco defines the IoT as a network of sensors that are attached to the objects and communication devices and provide data that can be analyzed and utilized for initiating automated actions [13]. Decision-making is dependent on when the objects can sense and when they can communicate. The IoT has been designated as a crucial component for business growth in terms of deploying IoT-enabled components or business strategies. It will speed up time-to-market, optimize asset utilization, improve supply-chain efficiency, optimize asset utilization, improve product development, and implement predictive maintenance.

1.3 EVOLUTION

Since its invention, the IoT has paved an eventful journey and has now become a powerful driver for the growth of businesses. Although the IoT is rapidly progressing, there is a need to look at the development of key fundamentals associated with the evolutionary process of the IoT and to understand in a better way how it entered into the current technological mainstream.

The concept of Internet connectivity began proliferating in the early 1990s when consumer markets and enterprises were in the growing stage. Kevin Ashton, who was the co-founder of Auto-ID Center at MIT, coined the term "Internet of Things" in the year 1999. The core idea was to identify and track the products more accurately using Radio Frequency Identification. Since then, numerous technologies have come into existence to support the growth of the IoT. Table 1.1 summarizes the milestones achieved during this evolutionary process.

TABLE 1.1   Events associated with the evolution of IoT

YEAR	EVENTS
1999	Kevin Ashton, executive director and co-founder of Auto-ID Center, coined the term Internet of Things (IoT); First Machine-to-Machine (M2M) protocol Message Queuing Telemetry Transport (MQTT) was developed.
2000	LG, a South Korean multi-national electronics company, announced its first Internet-connected refrigerator plan named Internet Digital DIOS, which used Local Area Network (LAN) port for Internet connectivity; idea of cloud computing came into existence.
2001	United States-based National Science Foundation established an Industry-University Cooperative Research Centre (IUCRC) for using IoT-based predictive analytics technology.
2002	Collaborative development of Near Field Communication Technology (NFCT) was announced by Philips and Sony.
2003–2004	Mainstream publications including *the Guardian, the Boston Globe, and Scientific American* mentioned the term the IoT.
2005	International Telecommunications Union (ITU) published its first report on the IoT.
2006	A Bluetooth smart technology wire was introduced by Nokia.
2007	European Research Cluster on IoT (IERC), a European Union based organization, was founded.
2008	First European IoT conference was organized; Internet-connected devices exceeded the number of people worldwide.
2009	Google started self-driving cars tests.
2010	ioBridge, an IoT company, developed the first online tide monitoring system.
2011	IoT Global Standards Initiative (GSI) was created; the term Industry 4.0 was revived.
2012	IPv6 was launched worldwide.
2013	Internet.org, a partnership between Nokia, Samsung, Ericsson, MediaTek, Opera Software, Qualcomm, and social networking service provider Facebook, was launched.
2014	IoT Incubation Council was launched.
2015	Internet of Things Security Foundation (IoTSF) was launched.
2016	DDoS attacks powered by IoT devices were conducted using Mirai malware.
2017	IoT Terms Database was created by IoT One, which is a reliable source containing information about the Industrial Internet of Things (IIoT).
2018	California became the first state to pass IoT cybersecurity law.
2019	Year for the 4th annual IoT Global Innovation Forum.

1.4 RELATED STATISTICS

At present, there are 26.66 billion connected IoT devices in the market for the year 2019, and every second 127 new devices are being connected to the Internet [14]. 40.2% of these devices are in use for business and manufacturing. Key areas include delivering real-time analytics of supply chains, providing diagnostic information about the equipment, and controlling the robotic machinery. Thirty and three tenths percent of IoT devices are a part of the healthcare industry for health monitoring and storing personal records safely. Eight and three tenths percent are a part of retail services including inventory tracking, providing online services to the clients, and consumer analytics. Seven and seven tenths percent are used in the security domain including remote sensing, biometric locks, and facial recognition. Four and one tenths percent are a part of the transportation industry including Global Positioning System (GPS) locators and performance tracking. Statistics also show that around 75% of the business-related IoT projects are facing failure due to limited internal expertise, time to completion, exceeding budget, and quality of data as some of the key reasons. Considering the global machine-to-machine (M2M) connections that are most commonly used in the commercial sector, 27% are in China, 29% are in Europe, 40% are in Asia, and 19% are in the United States.

Apart from delivering substantial benefits to the users, the IoT is facing unprecedented security challenges as well. The average financial damages caused by cyber attacks to businesses across the globe as of the year 2018 are shown in Figure 1.1 [15]. A survey showed that as of 2018, 38% of the organizations across the globe have adopted a set of security standards and constant monitoring techniques [16].

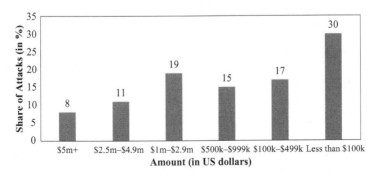

FIGURE 1.1   Global financial damages to businesses due to cyber attacks (as of April 2018).

1.5 INDUSTRIAL FORECASTS

In this section, we discuss some of the industrial forecasts for the IoT. Beginning with general anticipations, we will switch our attention to security-related predictions.

1.5.1 General Forecasts

According to Gartner's forecasts, usage of 14.2 billion connected things will be seen in the year 2019, and this will reach to 25 billion by the year 2021 [17]. Worldwide technology-wise spending on the IoT is estimated to reach $1.2 trillion by the year 2022, with a Compound Annual Growth Rate (CAGR) growth of 13.6% from 2017 to 2022 [18]. The sensor market is expected to progress through the year 2023, with newer applications, algorithms, and reduced prices. DBS Asian forecasts predict that the IoT installed base will experience a growth from 6.3 million units to 1.25 billion from the year 2016 to 2030 [19].

IoT Analytics predicts that the global market for the IoT will reach $1.56 trillion by the year 2025, and the market for industry 4.0 services and products will reach $310 billion by the year 2023 [20,21]. Statista predicted that by the year 2020, transportation and logistics, discrete manufacturing and utilities industries are expected to spend $40 billion on IoT systems, platforms, and services [22]. In addition, usage of 12.86 billion IoT devices and sensors in the consumer segment is expected by the year 2020, with a CAGR growth of 24.57% from the year 2017 [23]. The number of IoT devices are expected to reach 75.44 billion by the year 2025 [24]. Ericsson's forecast expects the number of cellular IoT connections to reach 3.5 billion by the year 2023 accompanied with a CAGR growth of 30% [25].

According the Gartner, the top ten strategic IoT technologies and trends would include artificial intelligence, social, legal, and ethical IoT, infonomics and data broking, intelligent mesh, IoT governance, sensor innovation, trusted hardware and operating systems, user experiences, silicon chip innovation, and wireless networking technologies [26].

1.5.2 Security-Related Forecasts

Security has become an inherent part of the IoT vision and architecture, and it is expected that security breaches will promote industries to come up with

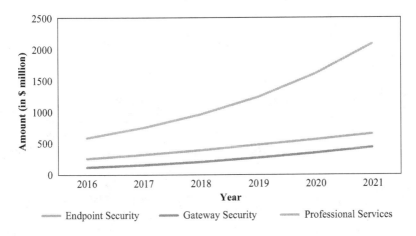

FIGURE 1.2 Global IoT security spending forecast.

more and enhanced security solutions. Although the exact influence of these predictions is accompanied with several questions, it will certainly help in shaping the industrial evolutionary process in the domain [27].

Gartner predicted that newer threats would come into the picture by the year 2021 with hackers finding novel ways for attacking IoT systems and protocols raising a requirement of hardware and software amendments [28]. It is also predicted that the investment in IoT endpoint security solutions would rise from $240 in the year 2016 to $631 million in the year 2021, accompanied with a CAGR growth of 21.38% [29]. Gateway security spending will reach from $102 in 2016 to $415 in 2021. Similarly, professional service securities will see an investment growth from $570 in 2016 to $2071 in 2021. Figure 1.2 shows the IoT security-spending forecast. Worldwide IoT security spending will reach $3.1 billion in the year 2021, with a CAGR growth of 27.87% from the year 2016 [30]. Size of the IoT security market from the year 2016 to 2025 across the globe is expected to reach $30.9 billion from $7.28 billion [31].

The smart home security segment is expected to achieve a revenue of $28.19 billion by the year 2023 across the globe [32]. Many hardware manufacturers including Dell, Cisco, and HPE, are developing specialized infrastructure for end-point security for preventing loss of data, ensuring threat protection and access control, enforcing right privileges, and so forth.

1.6 CHAPTER SUMMARY

Ubiquitous sensing, computing, and communication facilities provided by IoT are seeking attention of industries at various levels and in different sectors due to their significant impact on various aspects of our everyday lives. To understand its current state of being, it becomes necessary to outline the events associated with the journey of the IoT so far. This chapter began with a brief introduction to the IoT paradigm through various definitions and progressed toward highlighting the historical events associated with the development of this ground-breaking idea. Further sections presented the industrial statistics and forecasts related to the domain. In the next chapter, we will discuss the existing architectural concepts and business models associated with the IoT that would enlighten its workflow concepts.

REFERENCES

1. Tewari, A., & Gupta, B. B. (2017). A lightweight mutual authentication protocol based on elliptic curve cryptography for IoT devices. *International Journal of Advanced Intelligence Paradigms*, *9*(2–3), 111–121.
2. Stergiou, C., Psannis, K. E., Gupta, B. B., & Ishibashi, Y. (2018). Security, privacy & efficiency of sustainable cloud computing for big data & IoT. *Sustainable Computing: Informatics and Systems*, *19*, 174–184.
3. Tewari, A., & Gupta, B. B. (2018). Security, privacy and trust of different layers in Internet-of-Things (IoTs) framework. *Future Generation Computer Systems*. https://doi.org/10.1016/j.future.2018.04.027.
4. Gupta, B. B., & Quamara, M. (2018). An overview of Internet of Things (IoT): Architectural aspects, challenges, and protocols. *Concurrency and Computation: Practice and Experience*, e4946.
5. Gupta, B. B., & Sheng, Q. Z. (Eds.). (2019). *Machine learning for computer and cyber security: Principle, algorithms, and practices*. Boca Raton, FL: CRC Press.
6. Jiang, F., Fu, Y., Gupta, B. B., Lou, F., Rho, S., Meng, F., & Tian, Z. (2018). Deep learning based multi-channel intelligent attack detection for data security. *IEEE Transactions on Sustainable Computing*.
7. Gupta, B. B., & Agrawal, D. P. (Eds.). (2019). *Handbook of research on cloud computing and big data applications in IoT*. Hershey, PA: IGI Global.
8. Adat, V., & Gupta, B. B. (2018). Security in Internet of Things: Issues, challenges, taxonomy, and architecture. *Telecommunication Systems*, *67*(3), 423–441.
9. Voas, J., Kuhn, R., Laplante, P., & Applebaum, S. (2018). *Internet of Things (IoT) Trust Concerns* (No. NIST Internal or Interagency Report (NISTIR) 8222 (Draft)). Gaithersburg, MD: National Institute of Standards and Technology.

10. NIST. https://csrc.nist.gov/News/2016/Release-of-Special-Publication-800-183,-Network-of. Accessed April 2019.
11. Gartner. https://www.gartner.com/it-glossary/internet-of-things/. Accessed April 2019.
12. ITU. https://www.itu.int/en/ITU-T/gsi/iot/Pages/default.aspx. Accessed May 2019.
13. CISCO. https://www.cisco.com/c/en/us/about/press/internet-protocol-journal/back-issues/table-contents-57/153-internet.html. Accessed May 2019.
14. Safeatlast. https://safeatlast.co/blog/iot-statistics/. Accessed March 2019.
15. Statista. https://www.statista.com/statistics/881158/average-financial-damages-via-cyber-attacks/. Accessed April 2019.
16. Statista. https://www.statista.com/statistics/780553/worldwide-enterprise-iot-solutions-security-deployment/. Accessed April 2019.
17. Gartner.https://www.gartner.com/en/newsroom/press-releases/2018-11-07-gartner-identifies-top-10-strategic-iot-technologies-and-trends. Accessed February 2019.
18. Forbes. https://www.forbes.com/sites/louiscolumbus/2018/12/13/2018-roundup-of-internet-of-things-forecasts-and-market-estimates/#13db9a517d83. Accessed January 2019.
19. DBS Asian Insights. https://www.dbs.com/aics/pdfController.page?pdfpath=/content/article/pdf/AIO/062018/180625_insights_internet_of_things_the_pillar_of_artificial_intelligence.pdf. Accessed March 2019.
20. IoT Analytics. https://iot-analytics.com/state-of-the-iot-update-q1-q2-2018-number-of-iot-devices-now-7b/. Accessed December 2018.
21. IoT Analytics. https://iot-analytics.com/industry-4-0-and-smart-manufacturing/. Accessed December 2018.
22. Statista. https://www.statista.com/statistics/666864/iot-spending-by-vertical-worldwide/. Accessed April 2019.
23. Statista. https://www.statista.com/statistics/370350/internet-of-things-installed-base-by-category/. Accessed April 2019.
24. Statista. https://www.statista.com/statistics/471264/iot-number-of-connected-devices-worldwide/. Accessed April 2019.
25. Ericsson. https://www.ericsson.com/assets/local/mobility-report/documents/2018/ericsson-mobility-report-june-2018.pdf. Accessed April 2019.
26. Gartner. https://www.gartner.com/en/newsroom/press-releases/2018-11-07-gartner-identifies-top-10-strategic-iot-technologies-and-trends. Accessed April 2019.
27. I-Scoop. https://www.i-scoop.eu/internet-of-things-guide/iot-security-forecasts/. Accessed April 2019.
28. Gartner. http://www.gartner.com/newsroom/id/3221818. Accessed April 2019.
29. Gartner. https://www.gartner.com/en/newsroom/press-releases/2018-03-21-gartner-says-worldwide-iot-security-spending-will-reach-1-point-5-billion-in-2018. Accessed March 2019.
30. Gartner. https://www.gartner.com/document/3863770. Accessed April 2019.
31. Statista. https://www.statista.com/statistics/993789/worldwide-internet-of-things-security-market-size/. Accessed April 2019.
32. Statista. https://www.statista.com/statistics/645392/revenue-in-the-smart-home-segment-security-worldwide/. Accessed April 2019.

IoT Architecture and Business Models

2

2.1 INTRODUCTION

The Internet of Things (IoT) promises a plethora of opportunities to organizations that are seeking the integration of IoT products with their business processes. However, in reality, this idea is difficult to execute considering the number and diversity of devices along with the underlying conditions that are to be fulfilled in order to make this integration work. In simple terms, it demands the establishment of a reliable IoT architecture. Moreover, appropriate business models are required to be developed for providing a viable support to how IoT industries should operate [1–4].

Various organizations and research communities have proposed different architectural frameworks depending on different contexts. These include feature-oriented architectures (service-oriented [5], security-oriented [6], energy-efficient [7], quality of service [8]), component-oriented architectures (gateway-centric [9], user-centric [10], data-centric [11]), application-driven architectures [12,13], technology-driven architectures (Blockchain [14], software-defined networking [15], network function virtualization [16], machine-to-machine [17]), topology-specific architectures (centralized [18], distributed [19], hybrid), and so forth. The underlying building blocks including devices, protocols, and applications influence the applicability and effectiveness of these frameworks. In addition, to identify how to deliver products and services to the consumers, and to anticipate the expenses in order to make revenues, business models provide the right solution. However, no canonical business model for the IoT exists, which calls for the careful analysis of how consumers can derive value from the positioning of the services and the products in the IoT value-chain [20,21].

The next section presents an architectural framework for the IoT consisting of different layers and discusses the elements associated with these layers including the devices, functionalities, and various technologies involved. The layers are distinguished in order to track the overall consistency of IoT systems.

2.2 IoT ARCHITECTURE

IoT architecture can be described in terms of three layers – perception layer, transmission layer, and application layer. This architecture is flexible to incorporate more layers and is described as follows –

1. *Perception or Sensor Layer*: Having the responsibility of collecting information about the digitally connected things through its sensing capabilities, perception, or sensor layer acts as a bottom line of IoT infrastructure. This layer is analogous to the sensing capabilities of human beings. Digital environmental monitoring can be done through various heterogeneous sensing technologies including Near Field Communication, Radio Frequency Identification, etc., depending on the requirement of the application. This layer creates a collaborative network with the above layers by adopting an autonomous working mode.

   In addition to the main task of perceiving the features of the physical objects, this layer extends its capability through processing power. Two major processing technologies that play an eminent role in the perception layer are nanotechnology and embedded intelligence. Specifically, Micro-Electromechanical systems provide unprecedented features to the perception layer as they merge nanotechnology with nano-electromechanical systems. Micro-Electromechanical systems-featured microchips when embedded into physical world objects enable these objects to connect to the Internet in order to provide information. Embedded intelligence technology provides processing capability to the perception layer that is required by various applications.

2. *Network or Transmission Layer*: The data collected or processed by the perception layer are handled by the network layer. It acts as a medium of transmission for data between the perception layer and application layer with the help of wired or wireless technologies, hence, also referred to as the transmission layer. Another major responsibility of the network layer is to provide connectivity between networking devices and digital objects by creating a user-friendly network. Transmission media used by this layer include infrared technology, Bluetooth, Fiber to the x (FTTx), ZigBee, 3G/4G, Wireless Fidelity (Wi-Fi), and so forth. Since this layer processes or carries a huge amount of data, it also provides a middleware that is used to process and store this data. Cloud computing is one of the most preferable technologies that is used by the middleware, as it offers a dynamic and reliable interface for processing and storing the data.

3. *Application Layer*: If the perception layer is considered as the backbone of the IoT layered architecture, the application layer acts as the front end of this architecture. This layer uses the data processed by the perception and network layers. The major responsibility of this layer is to define applications that are either used or deployed by the IoT paradigm. These applications include smart forests, smart cities, smart homes, smart transportation, smart education, smart healthcare, and so forth. In some cases, this layer also provides actuator devices to the end users in order to exploit the full potential of IoT devices. To fulfill the vision of the IoT, every application is unique to facilitate the services as these are heterogeneous, and are based on the collected information and user's requirement. In addition to the offerings of these three layers, there are some additional aspects that work across the entire IoT architecture. These include scalability and security considerations, trust management, and network management and control [22–25]. Figure 2.1 shows the above-discussed IoT architecture [26].

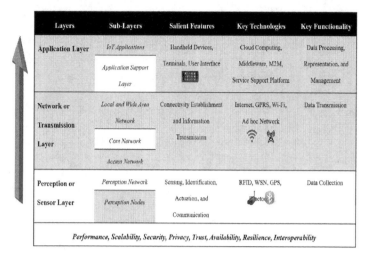

FIGURE 2.1 IoT architecture.

2.3 BUSINESS MODELS FOR IoT

In this section, we discuss business models with respect to the IoT in detail including the basic concepts, components, development challenges, and types along with the technological perspectives associated with them.

2.3.1 What Are Business Models?

Business models provide an overview of how companies and organizations should conduct their businesses. These involve –

1. Describing the values that companies offer to their customers that may belong to the same or different segments.
2. Defining the architecture of the firm along with its network consisting of partners for creating, marketing, delivering, and capturing these values, along with the relationship capital for generating revenues that may sustain for longer.

In other words, business models are the plan followed by companies for generating revenue from operations, and the success of companies highly depends on business models [27].

2.3.2 Components of Business Models

Business models comprise of different components that are shown in Figure 2.2 and discussed as follows [28] –

1. *Customer segments*: These include the type of customers that are targeted for selling the products. These may include a mass or niche market, diversified segments, and multi-sided platforms.
2. *Customer relationships*: These include the ways for establishing relationships with the target customers including personal or dedicated assistance, self-service, automated service, communities, and co-creation.
3. *Channels*: These include the ways of selling the products to the target customers including sales force, web sales, own or partner stores, and wholesaler.
4. *Revenue streams*: These include the ways of generating revenues that include asset sales, usage fees, subscription fees, start-up fees, installation fees, brokerage fees, renting or leasing, licensing, and advertising.
5. *Key activities and resources for producing and selling the product*: Key activities include customer and product development,

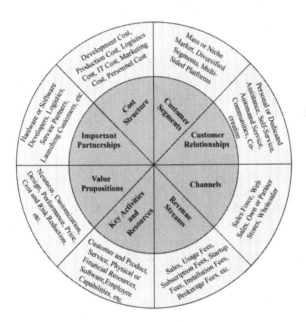

FIGURE 2.2 Components of business models.

implementation, service, marketing, sales platform and software development, partner management, and logistics. Key resources include physical or financial resources, software, intellectual property, employee capabilities, and relations.

6. *Value propositions*: These determine the value brought by the products that include newness, customization, design, performance, price, cost and risk reduction, convenience and comfort, usability, facility of amendments, and brand.

7. *Important partnerships*: These include hardware or software developers, distributors, suppliers, logistics, service partners, launching customers, and data interpreters.

8. *Cost structure*: It includes the ways through which cost is incurred including development cost, production cost, logistics cost, Information Technology (IT) cost, marketing or sales cost, and personnel cost.

2.3.3 Challenges in Developing Business Model Frameworks for the IoT

The challenges associated with the development of business models for the IoT ecosystem are discussed as follows [27,29] –

1. *Traditional business models*: Traditional or conventional business models are not as adequate for the IoT ecosystem as they are firm-centric. In addition, the diversity of entities demands the collaboration among industries. Hence, newer business models are desirable in order to facilitate the commercial exploitation of new IoT applications and to create value by ensuring financial returns. These models should be clear and widely accepted.

2. *Challenges associated with value propositions*: Value propositions are considered as one of the most significant building blocks for IoT business models apart from customer relationships and important partnerships. Cost reduction, being an important value proposition, is a part of business models in various companies. However, it is still not enough and requires businesses to extend from models associated with cost reductions in order to explore models associated with generating revenues. Other challenges related to value proposition include visualization, customer interaction, creating a dynamic offering portfolio, and articulated offering.

3. *Challenges associated with key partnerships*: It is now not possible to build independent solutions based on traditional business models,

and companies have to outsource the key activities associated with the product development with their partners. These partnerships are crucial in the sense that they create long-term relations, facilitate information sharing, and support joint cost reduction. However, it leads to increasing complexity in the development process, as a synchronization is required to be established between regulations and policies of partner companies.

4. *Lack of related research and empirical validation*: Research done in the field of IoT business models is relatively limited and many aspects are still unexplored. Moreover, the results already present a lack of empirical validation.

5. *Dynamic adoption*: Rapidly changing market ecosystems with respect to technology call for companies to adopt the changes and to address the challenges with the same pace that leads to the creation of win-win information exchange among stakeholders.

6. *Immature innovations*: Immature innovations that cannot be mapped to products or services also serve as a key challenge in the development of business models.

7. *Unstructured ecosystems*: These include ill-defined underlying structures, stakeholder roles, value-creating logics, and governance.

8. *Use of standards*: Inter-connecting various types of IoT devices without using emerging standards that are commonly accepted is also one of the key challenges in the development of business models.

9. *Application data handling*: Data generated by IoT devices are also accessed by the parties that provide market solutions. However, apart from bringing opportunities, it creates risks as well. The issues that are usually encountered are associated with the ownership of data, data usage, data replication, and so forth. Reliable implementation, transparency, and clarity in the conceptual aspects become challenging when multiple parties are involved with the same application.

10. *Mismatch in hardware and software culture*: A disruptive innovation strategy that is followed by many IoT solutions makes them difficult to be compared, and more often, they target a new market. Deciding whether software or hardware will be more dominative is a difficult task. Lack of quantitative and empirical research makes this problem even worse as fragmentary knowledge cannot provide the relevant answer. Hardware businesses are prone to high costs being incurred in case of a minor error in the product that has already been sold, which calls for damage control for their image. On the other hand, software businesses follow an agile development process in which even after the delivery to the customers, patches can be made and updates can be ensured at almost no additional cost.

11. *Optimal balance between product and service business*: Services and products are fundamentally different from each other. Achieving an optimal balance between their strategic and operational characteristics for determining development, sale, provisioning, categories, payment and pricing, revenue threshold, etc., is challenging.

2.3.4 IoT Business Models

Different IoT business models have been proposed in the literature that can be applied independently or in a group to increase the benefits. These are discussed as follows –

1. *Asset-sharing model*: Asset sharing is appropriate for situations where customers are using expensive products, but are not able to utilize the same to their maximum capacity. Automobile companies are making use of such business models to maximize their utilization across different customer bases such that each customer pays a reduced price per product, thereby achieving quick market penetration. Smart energy distribution systems can also make use of such models in which batteries can be deployed within the buildings for supplying power and the extra energy left unconsumed can be sold back to the smart grids. It would allow customers to pay less even if they are not using the extra capacity.

2. *Monetization of data*: The data collected by IoT devices are useful for deriving insights. Social networking companies like Facebook collect bulk data from the users, and this data provide value to the advertising companies for promoting products and services. In return, these companies make money. Similarly, other IoT products can provide value to the end users by deploying the IoT devices for data collection and by eliminating the cost of purchase for the end users. In return, the network is built that promotes attractive data proposition from the third parties as well. For instance, IoT devices can be used for monitoring driving habits of people, and the data collected by them are useful for insurance companies to identify driving patterns of many people at a time. An extension can be developed in which needs of the users can be resolved first, and then their data can be monitored for generating revenue. In order to avoid any conflict of interests, they should be informed about how their data will be used and by whom, while at the same time maintaining the privacy.

3. *Outcome-based model*: This model follows the approach of paying for the product benefits instead of the product itself. In this scenario, the

customers may prefer to use the services of the products by taking them on lease instead of paying the full amount in purchasing the product.

4. *Service offering*: As per this model, IoT products can be used to provide services to the customers, and hence, can be considered as an enabler or differentiator for the company. For instance, sensors can be deployed to monitor the machinery in an industry, for predicting maintenance, and so forth. Small buildings can be equipped with IoT devices for monitoring the rate of energy consumption.

5. *Subscription model*: This is a recurring-revenue model in which 24 * 7 connectivity of the IoT devices can be leveraged for generating continuous revenue. Instead of exploiting a one-time sale, revenue can be generated from the continuous value. Software products are mainly suitable for adopting this model. Paid upgrade can also be provided in the case where the underlying strategy supports it. It also promotes in establishing active relations with the customers, as features that are more valuable can be provided to the customers as per their needs. Examples of IoT applications using this model include predictive maintenance, monitoring, and so forth.

6. *Razor Blade model*: In this model, the idea is to design IoT products to promote the sale of other products. The IoT product can be sold at a cost (or loss) and minimum investment is made on it. The consumer is expected to never run out of the consumables by reordering the same, which generates value for the customer as well as vendor. For instance, printing devices use ink cartridges that are to be re-ordered in order to continue using the printers. Another instance is contextual shopping used by Amazon in which it facilitates the re-ordering of the same product when needed, thereby reducing the barrier between the sellers and the consumers [30].

7. *Pay-per-usage*: This model follows the approach of charging the customers whenever they are actively interacting with the IoT products.

2.3.5 Technological Perspective of Business Models

In this section, we discuss how different technological perspectives influence the development of business models in the IoT.

2.3.5.1 Industrial Context

It is crucial to reduce media breaks within companies due to many reasons [31]. These are generally prone to errors, as humans are not proficient to replicate simple, boring, and tiring tasks, and typically create errors. In addition, simultaneous manual processing of bulk data is not possible with significant speed. Moreover, media breaks cause errors and are more costly than the use of automated machines for completing the same tasks. Industry 4.0 or the fourth Industrial Revolution is expected to reduce the transactional costs that are a result of breaks in the physical and virtual world. Barcodes, audio control, keyboards, and other such methods enable a reduction in media breaks and, thus, reduce the transaction costs. The IoT with its advent is bringing substantial ways to reduce media breaks. Since physical world objects are equipped with processing, storage, sensing, actuators, and other such resources, the transaction costs reduce to zero. In addition, high-resolution data are turning into something economically more viable. The cost of data collection decreases significantly with an increase in the degree of detail. IoT technologies would facilitate real-time data collection with reduced or almost zero costs. Decreasing sensing costs will also increase the richness of data. Sensors with low cost can be deployed to collect environmental parameters with ease. In addition, the latest connectivity and geo-tracking standards are capable of allowing data collection independent of the location.

2.3.5.2 Blockchain

Currently, paid information exchange involves third parties [32]. For instance, a developer has to buy an account for purchasing sensor data from a sensor data company. It not only decreases the efficiency, but also increases the cost. Cryptocurrencies have become popular in the past few years as the underlying Blockchain technology creates a possibility of various peer-to-peer applications avoiding any intermediary oversight. It has lead to the development of various business models for the IoT for facilitating micro-payments. These business models aim at decentralized IoT infrastructure, the level of which can vary during the development process.

2.3.5.3 5G

The IoT is undergoing a transition from infrastructure-driven aspects to business-driven ones. A significant effort is being applied for defining sensors, gateways, base stations, radios, and other such elements. In the near future, numerous business opportunities can be anticipated. However, these opportunities are expected to revolve around the line of privacy and trust and will be strongly dependent on regulations and standards. With the advent of 5G communications, a significant increase in data rate, reduction in end-to-end latency, and improvement in coverage can be seen [33]. Hence, 5G holds the potential of fulfilling stringent communication requirements of IoT applications.

2.4 CHAPTER SUMMARY

In this chapter, we discussed the layered architectural framework for the IoT that covered various aspects including entities, functionalities, and technologies present at each layer. Moreover, we presented different business models for the IoT including their building blocks, challenges involved in their development, and the impact of different technological perspectives over them.

In the next chapter, we will discuss different development primitives for the IoT and their role in fostering the growth of this paradigm.

REFERENCES

1. Gupta, B. B. (Ed.). (2018). *Computer and cyber security: Principles, algorithm, applications, and perspectives.* Boca Raton, FL: CRC Press.
2. Stergiou, C., Psannis, K. E., Gupta, B. B., & Ishibashi, Y. (2018). Security, privacy & efficiency of sustainable cloud computing for big data & IoT. *Sustainable Computing: Informatics and Systems, 19,* 174–184.
3. Tewari, A., & Gupta, B. B. (2018). Security, privacy and trust of different layers in Internet-of-Things (IoTs) framework. *Future Generation Computer Systems.* https://doi.org/10.1016/j.future.2018.04.027.
4. Gupta, B. B., & Sheng, Q. Z. (Eds.). (2019). *Machine learning for computer and cyber security: Principle, algorithms, and practices.* Boca Raton, FL: CRC Press.
5. Issarny, V., Bouloukakis, G., Georgantas, N., & Billet, B. (2016, October). Revisiting service-oriented architecture for the IoT: A middleware perspective. In *International conference on service-oriented computing* (pp. 3–17). Cham, Switzerland: Springer.
6. Olivier, F., Carlos, G., & Florent, N. (2015). New security architecture for IoT network. *Procedia Computer Science, 52,* 1028–1033.
7. Kaur, N., & Sood, S. K. (2015). An energy-efficient architecture for the Internet of Things (IoT). *IEEE Systems Journal, 11*(2), 796–805.
8. Duan, R., Chen, X., & Xing, T. (2011, October). A QoS architecture for IOT. In *International conference on Internet of things and 4th international conference on cyber, physical and social computing* (pp. 717–720). IEEE.
9. Datta, S. K., Bonnet, C., & Nikaein, N. (2014, March). An IoT gateway centric architecture to provide novel M2M services. In *2014 IEEE World Forum on Internet of Things (WF-IoT)* (pp. 514–519). IEEE.
10. Datta, S. K., Gyrard, A., Bonnet, C., & Boudaoud, K. (2015, August). oneM2M architecture based user centric IoT application development. In *3rd international conference on future Internet of things and cloud* (pp. 100–107). IEEE.

11. Datta, S. K., Bonnet, C., Da Costa, R. P. F., & Härri, J. (2016, May). Datatweet: An architecture enabling data-centric IoT services. In *2016 IEEE region 10 symposium (TENSYMP)* (pp. 343–348). IEEE.
12. Catarinucci, L., De Donno, D., Mainetti, L., Palano, L., Patrono, L., Stefanizzi, M. L., & Tarricone, L. (2015). An IoT-aware architecture for smart healthcare systems. *IEEE Internet of Things Journal, 2*(6), 515–526.
13. Gaur, A., Scotney, B., Parr, G., & McClean, S. (2015). Smart city architecture and its applications based on IoT. *Procedia Computer Science, 52,* 1089–1094.
14. Novo, O. (2018). Blockchain meets IoT: An architecture for scalable access management in IoT. *IEEE Internet of Things Journal, 5*(2), 1184–1195.
15. Flauzac, O., González, C., Hachani, A., & Nolot, F. (2015, March). SDN based architecture for IoT and improvement of the security. In *2015 IEEE 29th international conference on advanced information networking and applications workshops* (pp. 688–693). IEEE.
16. Ojo, M., Adami, D., & Giordano, S. (2016, December). A SDN-IoT architecture with NFV implementation. In *2016 IEEE Globecom Workshops (GC Wkshps)* (pp. 1–6). IEEE.
17. Datta, S. K., Da Costa, R. P. F., Bonnet, C., & Härri, J. (2016, June). oneM2M architecture based IoT framework for mobile crowd sensing in smart cities. In *2016 European conference on networks and communications (EuCNC)* (pp. 168–173). IEEE.
18. Thota, C., Sundarasekar, R., Manogaran, G., Varatharajan, R., & Priyan, M. K. (2018). Centralized fog computing security platform for IoT and cloud in healthcare system. In *Fog computing: Breakthroughs in research and practice* (pp. 365–378). IGI Global.
19. Sarkar, C., Akshay Uttama Nambi, S. N., Prasad, R. V., Rahim, A., Neisse, R., & Baldini, G. (2014). DIAT: A scalable distributed architecture for IoT. *IEEE Internet of Things Journal, 2*(3), 230–239.
20. Jiang, F., Fu, Y., Gupta, B. B., Lou, F., Rho, S., Meng, F., & Tian, Z. (2018). Deep learning based multi-channel intelligent attack detection for data security. *IEEE Transactions on Sustainable Computing.*
21. Gupta, B. B., & Agrawal, D. P. (Eds.). (2019). *Handbook of research on cloud computing and big data applications in IoT.* Hershey, PA: IGI Global.
22. Adat, V., & Gupta, B. B. (2018). Security in Internet of things: Issues, challenges, taxonomy, and architecture. *Telecommunication Systems, 67*(3), 423–441.
23. Plageras, A. P., Stergiou, C., Kokkonis, G., Psannis, K. E., Ishibashi, Y., Kim, B. G., & Gupta, B. B. (2017, July). Efficient large-scale medical data (ehealth big data) analytics in internet of things. In *2017 IEEE 19th conference on business informatics (CBI)* (Vol. 2, pp. 21–27). IEEE.
24. Gupta, B., Agrawal, D. P., & Yamaguchi, S. (Eds.). (2016). *Handbook of research on modern cryptographic solutions for computer and cyber security.* Hershey, PA: IGI Global.
25. Tewari, A., & Gupta, B. B. (2017). Cryptanalysis of a novel ultra-lightweight mutual authentication protocol for IoT devices using RFID tags. *Journal of Supercomputing, 73*(3), 1085–1102.
26. Gupta, B. B., & Quamara, M. (2018). An overview of Internet of Things (IoT): Architectural aspects, challenges, and protocols. *Concurrency and computation: Practice and experience,* e4946.

27. Chan, H. C. (2015). Internet of things business models. *Journal of Service Science and Management, 8*(4), 552.
28. Dijkman, R. M., Sprenkels, B., Peeters, T., & Janssen, A. (2015). Business models for the Internet of Things. *International Journal of Information Management, 35*(6), 672–678.
29. Fleisch, E., Weinberger, M., & Wortmann, F. (2015). Business models and the internet of things. In *Interoperability and open-source solutions for the Internet of things* (pp. 6–10). Cham, Switzerland: Springer.
30. Tech.pinions. https://techpinions.com/battle-of-the-tablet-business-models-amazon-kindle-fire/10619. Accessed January 2019.
31. Gassmann, O., Frankenberger, K., and Csik, M. (2014). The business model navigator: 55 models that will revolutionise your business. *Financial Times.*
32. Zhang, Y., & Wen, J. (2017). The IoT electric business model: Using blockchain technology for the internet of things. *Peer-to-Peer Networking and Applications, 10*(4), 983–994.
33 Palattella, M. R., Dohler, M., Grieco, A., Rizzo, G., Torsner, J., Engel, T., & Ladid, L. (2016). Internet of things in the 5G era: Enablers, architecture, and business models. *IEEE Journal on Selected Areas in Communications, 34*(3), 510–527.

Communication and Development Primitives in IoT

3

3.1 INTRODUCTION

The idea of the Internet of Things (IoT) is related with connectivity and inter-operability, as discussed in the previous chapters. In the absence of these two elements, business value cannot be delivered. Various IoT solutions have been developed that rely on emerging networking technologies that are being adopted in order to ensure enhanced productivity. Moreover, communication needs to be established in a uniform way. To fulfill all these requirements, communication and development primitives are among one of the key solutions [1–4].

Communication protocols in the IoT facilitate pervasive coverage and are usually characterized by efficient interaction, advanced features, lower costs, and more security. In addition, standards and regulations define models and rules for communication in the IoT. With rapid change in technology, new design and developments tools are coming into the picture that target the developer community and have the potential to serve the requirements of the users. These tools not only remove the bottlenecks of the workflow, but also make the process fast.

In the next section, we present different IoT communication protocols, standards, and regulations in detail. We also present a comparative analysis of the two most commonly used application layer protocols, Message Queuing Telemetry Transport (MQTT) and Constrained Application Protocol (CoAP).

3.2 COMMUNICATION PROTOCOLS, STANDARDS, AND REGULATIONS

Communication protocols provide a language that allows devices and users to interact with each other in a more efficient and inter-connected manner. Table 3.1 enlists some of the popular protocols and their specific features as per the layered architecture of the IoT [5–7].

TABLE 3.1   Layer-wise IoT protocols

ARCHITECTURAL LAYER	PROTOCOL	SALIENT FEATURES
Perception and Sensor Layer (Physical and Data Link Layer)	Internet Protocol (IP)v6 over Low-Power Wireless Personal Area Networks (6LoWPAN) [8]	• Allows transmission of IPv6 packets over 802.15.4 links • Can be applied to small and low-power devices having processing constraints
	ZigBee [8]	• IEEE 802.15.3-based specification for low-power and low data rate PANs
Network or Transmission Layer (Internet Layer)	Routing Protocol for Low-Power and Lossy Networks (RPL) [9]	• Routing protocol designed for wireless networks that are susceptible to packet loss and have low power consumption
	Channel-Aware Routing Protocol (CARP) [10]	• Light-weight distributed routing protocol designed for underwater communication • Performs network initialization and data forwarding tasks

(Continued)

TABLE 3.1 (*Continued*)   Layer-wise IoT protocols

ARCHITECTURAL LAYER	PROTOCOL	SALIENT FEATURES
Application Layer	MQTT [11]	• Machine-to-Machine (M2M) communication-based publish-subscribe protocol for establishing light-weight connectivity over Transmission Control Protocol (TCP)
	CoAP [12]	• Request-response model-based protocol that runs over User Datagram Protocol (UDP) and is developed for resource-constrained environments
	Representational State Transfer (REST) [13]	• Request-response model-based protocol for developing web services
	Extensible Messaging and Presence Protocol (XMPP) [14]	• eXtensible Markup Language (XML)-based messaging protocol for multi-party chat, presence, instant messaging, audio and video calls, and content syndication
	Advanced Message Queuing Protocol (AMQP) [15]	• Publish-subscribe model-based messaging protocol with asynchronous communication capability • Possesses store-and-forward facility
	WebSocket [16]	• Protocol to facilitate communication channels over TCP • Follows handshake procedure to establish WebSocket sessions like Hyper-Text Transfer Protocol (HTTP)

Standards are the key to harmonize the interactions by defining how the inter-actions should take place and by optimizing the working of devices, protocols, platforms, and applications. Table 3.2 presents salient features of some of the standards designated for the IoT.

3.2.1 Message Queuing Telemetry Transport

It is described as a light-weight message-oriented application layer protocol designed for resource-constrained devices. It supports the following features:

TABLE 3.2   Standards for IoT

STANDARD	DESCRIPTION
IEEE 802.11ah [17]	• A version of Wi-Fi for low-power consumption devices • Operates in frequency bands lower than 1 GHz • Can be translated into long-range communication
Bluetooth Smart [18]	• A low-power version of Bluetooth for IoT devices • Facilitates longer range and mesh networking in which IoT devices act as communication node that relay communication to other nodes
Z-Wave [19]	• Licensed by Sigma Designs, it facilitates low-power mesh-networking • Operates at 908.42 MHz and supports 232 nodes
IEEE P2413 [20]	• Covers the fundamental definition of building blocks for IoT architecture and how they can be integrated with other multi-tiered systems
International Telecommunication Union Study Group 20 (ITU SG20) [21]	• Designed for smart cities to enable coordination in the development of IoT technologies including sensors networks and machine-to-machine communications
Industrial Internet Consortium (IIC) [22]	• Guidelines for industrial IoT applications
AllJoyn [23]	• Designed by Qualcomm, directs connectivity and service-layer operations for IoT devices for creating inter-operable products

- *Reliability*: It works over TCP and Internet Protocol and offloads reliability support on TCP. TCP ensures error-checking and ordered delivery of messages.
- *Topic-oriented Management*: It enables topic-oriented management and depends on a topic-based publish/subscribe model in which clients (such as sensor nodes) publish messages with a particular topic, and the clients that are subscribed to that particular topic receive the corresponding messages. These clients are connected with each other through a broker.
- *Symmetric Protocol*: MQTT can be considered as a symmetric protocol as both the clients and the broker can send or receive messages.
- *Light-weight Protocol*: It is designed in a manner to cause lower communication overhead. It supports lean header structure that reduces the packet parsing, making it suitable for resource-constrained IoT devices.
- *Security*: It is ensured through Transport Layer Security/Secure Socket Layer (TLS/SSL) that enables connection-oriented communication [24].
- *Scalability*: It permits a significant level of scalability options.
- *Diverse Applications*: It supports a diverse set of applications that belong to the IoT and M2M domain and are characterized by lower-latency, lower-channel bandwidth and power efficiency requirements. Automatic message forwarding makes MQTT a better option for these applications.
- *Message Retainment*: The broker keeps the messages that are already sent to the subscriber clients for broadcasting to the new subscribers of the same topic in the future.
- *Handling Disconnections*: It also supports automated mechanisms for managing the disconnections. The client nodes can also subscribe to a broker-side message (Last Will and Testament), and the broker sends the message to all the clients subscribed to this topic when an unexpected node disconnection is observed.
- *Multi-casting and Device-to-Device Transfer*: It does not support multi-casting of messages and device-to-device transfer.
- *Quality of Service (QoS)*: Three different QoS levels are defined to maintain the reliability of the message delivery and can be dynamically selected. These are given below.
  - *QoS level 0*: It corresponds to the messages that are delivered at most once without requiring the receipt of any acknowledgment. Moreover, the messages are not stored in the memory of

the sender client and, thus, can be duplicated or lost. However, it provides the fastest mode of delivering messages.

- *QoS level 1*: It corresponds to the messages that are delivered at least once and require receipt of delivery confirmation (PUBACK/SUBACK). These messages are stored by the clients locally to allow re-transmission in case of time-outs. However, it can also cause duplication of the messages that are being transmitted.
- *QoS level 2*: It corresponds to the messages that are delivered exactly once and are transmitted through a four-way handshake mechanism (PUBLISH, PUBACK, PUBREL, PUBCOMP) involving two-step acknowledgment. No duplication of messages can occur as the receiver client also stores the messages. It also avoids packet loss.

Another specification of MQTT, i.e., MQTT-SN, is available for constrained networks characterized by smaller packet lengths and low data rates. It runs over UDP and supports all the QoS levels, but without inheriting the transport layer's reliability property. Topic strings are replaced by topic IDs for content identification and reducing the complexity of the header.

3.2.2 Constrained Application Protocol

It is described as a light-weight application layer protocol designed for resource-constrained devices.

- *Request-Response Model*: It is based on REST architecture and works using a request-response model like HTTP.
- *Publish-Subscribe Model*: It also supports a publish-subscribe model based on a Universal Resource Identifier and extended GET method. Subscriber clients subscribe to resources indicated by Universal Resource Identifiers and are notified whenever a publisher client publishes data to those Universal Resource Identifiers.
- *Reliability*: CoAP provides its own reliability mechanism as UDP is not inherently reliable. Confirmable and non-confirmable messages are used for accomplishing the purpose. The former require an acknowledgment, this ensures reliability and corresponds to QoS level 1 of MQTT, whereas the latter does not require

an acknowledgment, does not guarantee reliability, and corresponds to QoS level 0 of MQTT. Another two options that are used include Acknowledgment and Reset.

- *QoS*: It does not provide any distinct QoS levels.
- *Security*: It uses Datagram TLS (DTLS) for ensuring security, which enables connection-less communication.
- *Content Negotiation*: It enables expressing an appropriate representation of a resource that allows for the independent evolution of clients and server, thereby adding newer representations without affecting one another.
- *Fragmentation*: It enables transmission of larger protocol data units in a block-wise manner.

Table 3.3 outlines the comparison of MQTT and CoAP [25].

TABLE 3.3   Comparison of MQTT and CoAP

COMPARISON PARAMETER	MQTT	CoAP
Underlying Transport Layer	TCP	UDP
Reliability Technique	3 QoS levels	Confirmable and non-confirmable messages
Avoidance of Duplication of Messages	QoS level 3	No provision
Underlying Working Model	Publish-Subscribe	Request-Response, Publish-Subscribe (Observe)
Transmission Delay	Performs better with lower packet loss rate	Performs better with higher packet loss rate
Methods used for Functionality	Connect, Disconnect, Publish, Subscribe, Unsubscribe, Close	Get, Put, Put, Delete
Security	TLS/SSL	DTLS
Content Format	Data-centric	Document-centric
Caching of Messages	No provision	Supports
Retention of Messages	Supports	No provision
Connection durability	Supports	No provision
Wills	Supports	No provision
Fragmentation	No provision	Supports
Discovery Mechanism	No provision	Supports

3.3 DESIGN AND DEVELOPMENT TOOLS

IoT design and development tools are the solutions that target the developer community for creating IoT applications. These tools consist of different types including software development kits (SDKs), integrated development environments (IDEs), libraries, frameworks, etc. Table 3.4 presents different tool categories along with some examples and salient features.

TABLE 3.4   Design and development tools for IoT

CATEGORY	EXAMPLE	DESCRIPTION
Hardware	Tessel 2 [26]	• Development board for holding modules, such as camera, RFID, accelerometer, and GPS • Can be programmed using Node.js • Contains on-board Wi-Fi facilities
	Kinoma Create [27]	• A device for connecting other devices for developing small applications including temperature sensors, movement sensors, and so forth
	BeagleBoard [28]	• Credit-card-sized computer for running Android and Linux-based applications • Has low power requirements and open-source hardware and software
Middleware	OpenIoT [29]	• Open-source middleware for obtaining information sensor clouds, thus enabling sensing-as-a-service
	IoTSyS [30]	• Provides communication stack for IoT devices and supports multiple protocols and standards
Operating System	Contiki [31]	• Open-source Operating System (OS) for the IoT that establishes connectivity among low-power microcontrollers through the Internet
	Raspbian [32]	• Credit-card-sized computer based on Debian distribution of Linux

(Continued)

TABLE 3.4 (Continued)   Design and development tools for IoT

CATEGORY	EXAMPLE	DESCRIPTION
Development Tools	Node-RED [33]	• Visual tool for wiring hardware devices, Application Programming Interface (APIs), and online services together in different ways • Built on Node.js and can run on Raspberry Pi
	M2MLabs Mainspring [34]	• Open-source application framework for developing M2M applications including remote monitoring, smart grid, and so forth • Facilitates device configuration, flexible monitoring of devices, data validation, and normalization
Platform and Integration Tools	PlatformIO [35]	• Open-source development ecosystem with unified debugger and cross-platform Integrated Development Environment (IDE) • Facilitates remote firmware updates and unit testing
	Arduino [36]	• Open-source electronics platform with easy-to-use software and hardware • Hardware board is capable of taking input (light, text message, finger touch) and maps it into corresponding output (turning on an Light Emitting Diode [LED], publishing online, motor activation) using the Arduino programming language
	DeviceHive [37]	• Open-source M2M communication framework with a cloud-based API that can be remotely controlled
	Eclipse IoT [38]	• Different projects for IoT development including application frameworks, services, IoT protocol implementations, and Lua-based tool • These projects include Paho, Mihini, and Koneki
	ThingSpeak [39]	• Open-source data platform for processing HTTP requests, storing, and processing data • Supports open API, plugins, and real-time data collection

(Continued)

TABLE 3.4 (*Continued*)   Design and development tools for IoT

CATEGORY	EXAMPLE	DESCRIPTION
Application-Specific Software	Home automation software (Home Assistant) [40]	• Open-source tool for home automation based on Python • Develops IoT systems that can be controlled remotely with desktop or mobile browsers
	Open Supervisory Control And Data Acquisition (SCADA) [41]	• Part of SCADA project and platform independent • Supports front and back-end applications along with editing and debugging facility

3.4 DATASETS

Various open-source datasets are available for experimentation and development in the IoT that allow developers to validate and enhance the functionality of the methodologies developed by them. These datasets are mostly sensor-based, collected through Internet-based protocols, and are general or application specific (security incidents, healthcare domains, weather, transportation, and so forth). These are summarized in Table 3.5.

TABLE 3.5   Datasets for IoT development

DATASET	TYPE	DESCRIPTION	INSTANCES
Linked Sensor Data (Kno.e.sis) [42]	Stand-alone repository	Datasets created by Kno.e.sis Center for sensors and sensor observations, and transformed from weather data (temperature, pressure, humidity, precipitation, wind speed, visibility) at MesoWest, United States	20,000 weather stations, 160 million observations

(Continued)

TABLE 3.5 (Continued)   Datasets for IoT development

DATASET	TYPE	DESCRIPTION	INSTANCES
Trajectory data collected from mobile GPS (Microsoft) [43]		Collected in GeoLife project by 182 users in a period of 3 years	17,621 trajectories
NPTLab [44]		Contains data associated with the Google+ users who link their Twitter or Facebook profile available publicly	Dynamic
Eurostat [45]		Contains information of security incidents against Information and Communication Technologies (ICT) and their repercussions	11680
Japan Traffic Flow [46]		Contains records of passengers and cargo collected through transportation in Japan	Passenger flow: 51 regions, cargo flow: 54 regions
A Community Resource for Archiving Wireless Data At Dartmouth (CRAWDAD) [47]	Multi-dataset repository	Wireless network data resource for researchers, collected from many contributing locations for analysis	Dynamic
UCI Machine-Learning Repository [48]		Collection of databases used by machine learning community for analyzing machine learning algorithms	Dynamic
Kaggle [49]		Collection of datasets published by users and research communities to work in collaboration	Dynamic

3.5 CHAPTER SUMMARY

In this chapter, we outlined various development primitives for the IoT including communication protocols, standards, and regulation, along with various design and development tools and datasets for conducting research and development in the domain.

In the next chapter, we will discuss various underlying technologies for the development of the IoT and their role in enhancing business productivity and consumer satisfaction in the domain.

REFERENCES

1. Gupta, B. B. (Ed.). (2018). *Computer and cyber security: Principles, algorithm, applications, and perspectives.* Boca Raton, FL: CRC Press.
2. Stergiou, C., Psannis, K. E., Gupta, B. B., & Ishibashi, Y. (2018). Security, privacy & efficiency of sustainable cloud computing for big data & IoT. *Sustainable Computing: Informatics and Systems, 19,* 174–184.
3. Tewari, A., & Gupta, B. B. (2018). Security, privacy and trust of different layers in Internet-of-Things (IoTs) framework. *Future Generation Computer Systems.* https://doi.org/10.1016/j.future.2018.04.027.
4. Gupta, B. B., & Sheng, Q. Z. (Eds.). (2019). *Machine learning for computer and cyber security: Principle, algorithms, and practices.* Boca Raton, FL: CRC Press.
5. Gupta, B. B., & Agrawal, D. P. (Eds.). (2019). *Handbook of research on cloud computing and big data applications in IoT.* Hershey, PA: IGI Global.
6. Adat, V., & Gupta, B. B. (2018). Security in Internet of Things: Issues, challenges, taxonomy, and architecture. *Telecommunication Systems, 67*(3), 423–441.
7. Plageras, A. P., Stergiou, C., Kokkonis, G., Psannis, K. E., Ishibashi, Y., Kim, B. G., & Gupta, B. B. (2017, July). Efficient large-scale medical data (ehealth big data) analytics in internet of things. In *2017 IEEE 19th conference on business informatics (CBI)* (Vol. 2, pp. 21–27). IEEE.
8. Mulligan, G. (2007, June). The 6LoWPAN architecture. In *Proceedings of the 4th workshop on embedded networked sensors* (pp. 78–82). ACM.
9. Accettura, N., Grieco, L. A., Boggia, G., & Camarda, P. (2011, April). Performance analysis of the RPL routing protocol. In *2011 IEEE international conference on mechatronics* (pp. 767–772). IEEE.
10. Basagni, S., Petrioli, C., Petroccia, R., & Spaccini, D. (2015). CARP: A channel-aware routing protocol for underwater acoustic wireless networks. *Ad Hoc Networks, 34,* 92–104.

11. Hunkeler, U., Truong, H. L., & Stanford-Clark, A. (2008, January). MQTT-S—A publish/subscribe protocol for wireless sensor networks. In *2008 3rd international conference on communication systems software and middleware and workshops (COMSWARE'08)* (pp. 791–798). IEEE.
12. Bormann, C., Castellani, A. P., & Shelby, Z. (2012). CoAP: An application protocol for billions of tiny internet nodes. *IEEE Internet Computing, 16*(2), 62–67.
13. Drytkiewicz, W., Radusch, I., Arbanowski, S., & Popescu-Zeletin, R. (2004, October). pREST: A REST-based protocol for pervasive systems. In *2004 IEEE international conference on mobile ad-hoc and sensor systems (IEEE Cat. No. 04EX975)* (pp. 340–348). IEEE.
14. Saint-Andre, P. (2011). *Extensible messaging and presence protocol (XMPP): Core*. Fremont, CA: Internet Engineering Task Force (IETF).
15. Vinoski, S. (2006). Advanced message queuing protocol. *IEEE Internet Computing*, (6), 87–89.
16. Pimentel, V., & Nickerson, B. G. (2012). Communicating and displaying real-time data with WebSocket. *IEEE Internet Computing, 16*(4), 45–53.
17. Adame, T., Bel, A., Bellalta, B., Barcelo, J., & Oliver, M. (2014). IEEE 802.11 AH: The WiFi approach for M2M communications. *IEEE Wireless Communications, 21*(6), 144–152.
18. Decuir, J. (2013). Introducing Bluetooth smart: Part 1: A look at both classic and new technologies. *IEEE Consumer Electronics Magazine, 3*(1), 12–18.
19. Fouladi, B., & Ghanoun, S. (2013). Security evaluation of the Z-Wave wireless protocol. *Black Hat USA, 24*, 1–2.
20. Logvinov, O., Kraemer, B., Adams, C., Heiles, J., Stuebing, G., Nielsen, M. L., & Mancuso, B. (2016). Standard for an architectural framework for the Internet of Things (IoT) IEEE p. 2413. Tech. Rep. September, 2016.
21. Um, T. W., Lee, G. M., & Choi, J. K. (2016). Strengthening trust in the future social-cyber-physical infrastructure: An ITU-T perspective. *IEEE Communications Magazine, 54*(9), 36–42.
22. Industrial Internet Consortium. Industrial Internet Consortium. *Industrial Internet Consortium official website*. http://www.iiconsortium.org/. Accessed September 14, 2016.
23. Villari, M., Celesti, A., Fazio, M., & Puliafito, A. (2014, November). AllJoyn Lambda: An architecture for the management of smart environments in IoT. In *2014 international conference on smart computing workshops* (pp. 9–14). IEEE.
24. Gupta, B. B., Gupta, S., & Chaudhary, P. (2017). Enhancing the browser-side context-aware sanitization of suspicious HTML5 code for halting the DOM-based XSS vulnerabilities in cloud. *International Journal of Cloud Applications and Computing (IJCAC), 7*(1), 1–31.
25. Thangavel, D., Ma, X., Valera, A., Tan, H. X., & Tan, C. K. Y. (2014, April). Performance evaluation of MQTT and CoAP via a common middleware. In *2014 IEEE ninth international conference on intelligent sensors, sensor networks and information processing (ISSNIP)* (pp. 1–6). IEEE.
26. Tessel. https://tessel.io. Accessed May 2019.
27. http://embedded-computing.com/news-id/?50159.
28. Beagleboard. http://beagleboard.org. Accessed May 2019.
29. OpenIoT. http://www.openiot.eu. Accessed May 2019.

30. TUWIEN. http://www.iue.tuwien.ac.at/cse/index.php/projects/120-iotsys-internet-of-things-integration-middleware.html. Accessed May 2019.
31. Contiki-os. http://www.contiki-os.org. Accessed March 2019.
32. Raspberrypi. https://www.raspberrypi.org/downloads/raspbian/. Accessed March 2019.
33. Nodered. https://nodered.org. Accessed March 2019.
34. M2Mlabs. http://www.m2mlabs.com. Accessed March 2019.
35. Platformio. https://platformio.org. Accessed March 2019.
36. Arduino. https://www.arduino.cc. Accessed April 2019.
37. Devicehive. https://devicehive.com. Accessed April 2019.
38. IoT.Eclipse. https://iot.eclipse.org. Accessed April 2019.
39. ThingSpeak. https://thingspeak.com. Accessed April 2019.
40. Home Assistant. https://www.home-assistant.io. Accessed April 2019.
41. OpenSCADA. http://oscada.org. Accessed April 2019.
42. LinkedSensorData. http://wiki.knoesis.org/index.php/LinkedSensorData. Accessed March 2019.
43. https://www.microsoft.com/en-us/download/details.aspx?id=52367&from=https%3A%2F%2Fresearch.microsoft.com%2Fen-us%2Fdownloads%2Fb16d359d-d164-469e-9fd4-daa38f2b2e13%2F.
44. Internet of People, Things and Computers. http://nptlab.di.unimi.it. Accessed April 2019.
45. Eurostat. https://ec.europa.eu/eurostat. Accessed April 2019.
46. National Land Numeric Information. http://nlftp.mlit.go.jp/ksj-e/jpgis/datalist/KsjTmplt-S05-d.html. Accessed September 2018.
47. Crawdad. https://crawdad.org. Accessed April 2019.
48. UCI Machine Learning Repository. https://archive.ics.uci.edu/ml/index.php. Accessed April 2019.
49. Kaggle. https://www.kaggle.com. Accessed April 2019.

Challenges in IoT

4

4.1 INTRODUCTION

The groundbreaking potential of the IoT is drawing the attention of many enterprises and industries across the globe. The successful implementation of the IoT is greatly influenced by the significant investments across different sectors, and its demand is continuously increasing. However, despite the opportunities the IoT provides and the necessary improvements done in the field so far, IoT adoption and expansion are still facing potential challenges that are widespread along the IoT chain (from physical devices as endpoints via network channels to the data consumers and holders) [1–3]. These challenges are summarized in Table 4.1 and are discussed in detail in the following sections [4].

4.2 CHALLENGES ASSOCIATED WITH IoT ARCHITECTURE

IoT architecture possesses challenges associated with its layers and their integration [5–7]. These are classified into two categories and are discussed as follows:

1. *Inter-layer challenges*: Cross-layer integration issues arise due to the high heterogeneity possessed by the layers of IoT architecture [8]. End users are facilitated by the data collection capabilities from the sensor nodes placed in different locations through applications designed for the purpose. These data in turn pass through the

TABLE 4.1 Challenges in the IoT

CATEGORY	CHALLENGE		EXAMPLE
IoT Architecture	Inter-layer		Heterogeneity, Data standardization, Data mapping, Integration of working, Complexity
	Intra-layer	Perception Layer	Difficulty of implementing security mechanisms, Physical damages, Malicious attacks, Node authentication, Data integrity
		Transmission Later	Device identification, Network congestion, Security attacks, Information disclosure, Malware intrusion, Phishing
		Application Layer	Information disclosure, Query and location privacy, Service interruption, Limited computation capabilities
Entities	Hardware		Physical damage to devices, Link interception, Integration of functionality
	Software		Degree of trust establishment and maintenance, Complex design process and software, Resource consumption, Operational cost, Fragmented requirements
	Data		Data sensitivity, Data and source authentication, Data corruption, Malicious data, Data processing, Bulk data generation, Unstructured data extraction and storage, Data capturing, Data transformation, Runtime anomalies, Data translation, Legacy systems, High costs
Technology-oriented	Specific to the IoT		Unique identification of devices, Global distribution of services, Durability of technical environment
	Related challenges	Wireless Sensor Network (WSN)	Secure routing, Architecture, Quality of Service (QoS), Energy optimization
		Cloud Computing	QoS, Data isolation, Efficient resource management, Scalability, Reliability, Recovery

(Continued)

TABLE 4.1 (Continued)   Challenges in the IoT

CATEGORY	CHALLENGE	EXAMPLE
Features	Security	Malware ingestion, Digital burglary, Data breaches, Exposure of sensitive data, Exploitation of device similarity, Type-specific challenges
	Privacy	Integrated used of consumer devices, Monitoring of user's activities, Global deployment of devices leading to cross-cultural differences
	Trust	Bulk usage of IoT devices, Lack of transparency
	Compatibility	Stand-alone legacy systems, Configuration management, Diversity in protocols, algorithms, and data
	Connectivity	Lack of network coverage, Legacy devices
	Capacity	Resource constrained devices, Embedding of functionality
	Scalability	Legacy systems, Device updating
	Longevity	Obsolete technologies
	Implementation Time and Cost	Device connection and functioning, Budget for large-scale environment
Development Practices	Standards	Poor design and configuration of devices, Bulk of devices
	Regulations	Cross-nation data flow, Civil rights, Data retention, Destruction policies, Legal liability, Complex regulatory analysis process
	Automation	Code error, Poorly designed algorithm
	Intelligent Analytics	Inaccurate analysis, Legacy systems

transmission layer of the network. The data can be collected through different ways, in different formats, by utilizing different protocols, and can be utilized for different purposes. Data standardization and mapping as per the layers are required in such scenarios. Incorrect integration methodologies may lead to data corruption or destruction. In addition, each layer of the IoT architecture utilizes different mechanisms to ensure validity, security, and privacy of the information, which in turn leads to increasing complexity. Cross-layer optimization techniques are relevant for such scenarios. IoT devices at different layers have different resource requirements and functionalities. For instance, sensors are deployed to collect data from the surroundings that is of few kilobytes, while high-end servers are responsible for aggregating the data collected by these sensors for processing and storage. Therefore, to ensure correct integrated working of these devices, these requirements and functionalities should be carefully taken into consideration.

2. *Intra-layer challenges*: Different layers of IoT architecture possess their own challenges [9]. Perception layer devices being resource-constrained in terms of processing power, energy, and storage are difficult to manage with respect to integration of conventional security mechanisms with data capturing capabilities. Since they are usually deployed in diverse environmental conditions, they are susceptible to physical damages. Massive level attacks such as distributed denial of service attacks, and other such intentional and malicious attempts, can lead to the manipulation of their operational parameters. Hence, to ensure that no physical event or malicious activity can disturb their standard functionality is challenging. Node authentication and data integrity are some other challenging issues. Compromised nodes can lead to the production of false results and unauthorized access to the information.

A transmission layer that is mainly comprised of the Internet is accessed by a bulk of IoT devices. In such scenarios, the unique identification of devices along with network congestion are difficult to handle. Distributed denial of service, information disclosure, malware intrusion, phishing, etc., add up to existing challenges. Security challenges due to heterogeneous fusion may also arise.

An application layer is comprised of applications associated with businesses or individuals, which are accompanied with various security and non-security issues including information disclosure, threat to query and location privacy, service interruption, etc. The limited computational capabilities of the smart devices supporting access to these applications also limit their capabilities.

4.3 CHALLENGES ASSOCIATED WITH ENTITIES

Different system entities including hardware, software, and data offer different challenges to the IoT that are discussed below:

1. *Hardware*: Physical devices, such as data storage devices, hardware tokens, Internet appliances, and servers that have embedded software and provide remote application services, require protection against physical damages including natural disasters as well as intentional malicious attempts [10]. Wired communication channels that carry information from sensors nodes till the consumption point can be intercepted, and hence, safety of these links is equally important. Another challenge is to integrate functionalities over resource-constrained hardware devices.

2. *Software*: Software typically includes application software having a specific purpose, such as communication, security, etc., and system software, such as operating systems, Database Management System (DBMS), etc., that are involved in the development and realization of application software. With a bulk of heterogeneous devices working together, the degree of trust is low, and hence, may provide an opportunity to the attacker to interfere with the normal workflow of the underlying software [11]. Since the IoT encompasses devices with diverse characteristics, such as sensors, actuators, and other connectivity solutions, a one-size-fits-all model cannot be applied to the software designing process. In addition, the complexity of the software is highly dependent on the nature of the task to be performed including data perception, storage, processing, security, and so forth. Resource consumption and overall operational cost of the system increase with the increasing size of the software. In such a scenario, the development of low-cost and low-power solutions for the resource-constrained IoT environment, while at the same time ensuring the fulfillment of the fragmented requirements, becomes challenging and requires a novel design methodology and appropriate engineering decisions.

3. *Data*: Data in a digital environment are the primary and crucial user assets that require efficient protection [12]. They may belong to an individual or an organization and may possess varying levels of content sensitivity as per the usage. For instance, health records of a patient or travel records of a person are more sensitive in comparison

to the environmental conditions of a city in terms of privacy. In an IoT environment where devices in bulk are operating, data and source authentication becomes challenging. Moreover, corrupted or malicious data when pushed into the network can create havoc.

Data processing in a resource-constrained ecosystem where devices are characterized with limited processing power is another challenging aspect and calls for the development of lightweight schemes for securing the devices. Bulk data generation, also termed as big data, is another open area of research with respect to the IoT domain. The growing number of connected devices are also a source of unstructured data generation, and it becomes challenging for the organizations to identify valuable data out of it all. Storage and retrieval of unstructured data are also complex tasks. Latest frameworks such as Hadoop and Cassandra have reduced the complexity of handling unstructured data to some extent. Ensuring correct data capturing capabilities is another challenging aspect that involves the collection of data from various sources, such as sensors, and transforming the data to a standard format in order to analyze and automate the data. Runtime anomalies such as power surges may lead to incorrect data being recorded. Moreover, translating data into meaningful information requires intelligent analytics. However, legacy systems can limit the capabilities of handling real-time data in bulk, as not all the data can be loaded at once. Higher costs also prevent adoption of new analytics technology.

4.4 TECHNOLOGY-ORIENTED CHALLENGES

The IoT as well as underlying technologies possess different challenges that are discussed as below:

1. *Challenges specific to the IoT*: The core idea of the IoT is to establish anytime and anywhere connectivity among the things via the Internet. Supporting a bulk of Internet-connected devices and assigning a unique identity to these devices is challenging. The concept of IPv6 ensures the scalability of the IoT and thus is considered as one of the solutions toward the identification of a bulk of IoT devices. However, Internet Protocol version 6 (IPv6) comes with its own concerns including topology variations, device mobility issues, node miniaturization, and so forth. Trade-offs between the global distribution of services and the durability of the technical environment call for novel regulatory methodologies.

2. *Challenges due to other related technologies*: The IoT is highly dependent on various other technologies including WSN, Radio Frequency Identification (RFID), Wi-Fi, distributed computing, cloud computing, GPS, and so forth, right from the construction of network till the execution of its functionalities. Since the Internet provides the basic framework for the IoT, challenges associated with it would play an important role in its development. WSN comes with challenges including secure routing protocols, architecture, QoS, energy optimization, and so forth [13]. Cloud computing brings issues such as QoS, data isolation, efficient resource management, scalability, reliability, recovery, and so forth [14].

4.5 CHALLENGES ASSOCIATED WITH FEATURES

These challenges are associated with the different features or attributes associated with the IoT and are discussed as below:

1. *Security*: Security is the foundational aspect of Internet-based applications, and hence, is perceived to be essential and one of the significant challenges for the IoT [15]. With different IoT devices proliferating at an exponential rate, attackers are gaining more opportunities to exploit the security loopholes through malware ingestion, digital burglary, data breaches, and so forth. Moreover, sensitive data associated with these devices when exposed can put people's privacy at stake. Similar kinds of devices in bulk can become victims of the exploitation of a single security vulnerability, and it is also challenging to deal with the type-specific challenges. Hence, a collaborative approach and component-level security along with cost and security trade-off analysis are in demand. Industries are required to leverage modern technologies to overcome these issues. Struggling to secure the data flow, establishing appropriate mechanisms to recognize, authenticate, and manage the device endpoints, understanding the nature of data collection and how data will be processed, and event management systems, are some of the means to counter these hurdles [16–19].
2. *Privacy*: The IoT ecosystem is accompanied with data privacy challenges that are different from the current privacy-related challenges [20]. Consumer devices, such as smart phones, home

appliances, vehicles, and so forth, are being used in integration that makes these issues more prevalent. Voice and face recognition mechanisms are being used for the identification of users, and the data corresponding to it are sent to the third parties or the cloud through which they can watch user's activities. The global deployment of IoT devices also faces cross-cultural boundaries where the meaning of privacy protection mechanisms may change drastically. Hence, to establish individual-specific privacy measures and fulfilling the organizational demands is challenging.

3. *Trust*: Though IoT devices are being used in bulk to make people's lives more convenient, these are also leading to some trust issues in the way businesses are using them to collect and process consumer-specific data [21]. Lack of transparency is one of the promoting factors toward this issue. Ensuring more visibility across the data practices and increasing the transparency of the data management and governance are some of the ways through which trust values can be enhanced among users.

4. *Compatibility*: Legacy systems are still operating as stand-alone systems rather than fully integrated ones, as they were not designed to be inter-operable, which is one of their biggest IoT implementations [22]. Managing the configuration process is complex and time-consuming, and hence, requires careful planning, standardized configuration interface, methods, and tools. It becomes trickier for engineers to consider the abovementioned factors at the same time while designing new and advanced systems. Different mechanical, electronic, electrical, and processing devices operate on different protocols, execute different algorithms, and accept data of diverse nature as input that makes the compatibility issues an important concern.

5. *Connectivity*: Lack of Internet connectivity in many areas gives rise to networking challenges [23]. Logistics and transport companies that are always engaged in remote operations demand powerful and reliable communication networks in order to collect the data even in rough situations and transmit the data for the purpose of analysis. Physical devices such as routers influence the quality of signals being transmitted. Moreover, diverse technologies facilitate fast communication. However, an increase in the inter-connected devices at a rate much higher than the overall network coverage makes the monitoring and tracking problems more difficult. In addition, legacy devices do not support the latest technologies. For instance, conventional devices depend on telemetry systems, programmable logic controllers, remote terminal units for generating data, whereas IoT devices are compatible with Wi-Fi, Local Area Network (LAN), General Packet Radio Service (GPRS), and so forth.

6. *Capacity*: IoT devices are characterized by a resource-constrained nature, and hence, have limited capacities in terms of battery power, processing power, memory, and so forth [24]. Embedding the device-specific functionalities is becoming challenging in this context.

7. *Scalability*: To ensure the efficient growth of business, the scalability factor is of paramount importance [25]. Moreover, it is required to be fulfilled without interfering with the already existing systems and causing system shutdown. System design should be made by leaving enough room to incorporate amendments instead of re-designing the entire system.

8. *Longevity*: As the IoT is an integration of technologies, and some of them are expected to eventually become obsolete in the coming years, the devices using them will become useless. Since IoT devices usually tend to have a longer life-span and are designed to function in the absence of the support, ensuring longevity is challenging in this context.

9. *Implementation Time and Cost*: One of the common hurdles to overcome with respect to IoT devices is the time taken to establish connectivity among these devices and their functionality. IoT sensors are equipped with limited assets that can provide limited benefits only. Moreover, the cost of IoT deployment for large-scale scenarios is usually very high.

4.6 CHALLENGES ASSOCIATED WITH DEVELOPMENT PRACTICES

Challenges associated with development practices and their influence in the IoT are discussed as below:

1. *Standards*: The potential of IoT devices is limited by a lack of standards and best practices [26]. Standards guide the manufacturers and developers to design products with already defined parameters. However, in the absence of the standards, the devices may operate in a disruptive manner when connected through the Internet and may have an undesired impact. Poorly designed and configured devices can also have unwanted consequences on other devices in the network. A large number of IoT devices add the difficulty of managing and configuring the devices, making the thoughtful standardization of tools, methodologies, and interfaces an essential aspect.

2. *Regulations*: The IoT is surrounded by a wide range of legal and regulatory questions, as the technological advancement is more rapid than the corresponding policies and regulations [27]. Legal issues including cross-nation data flow, civil rights, data retention, destruction policies, and legal liability are difficult to maintain with a large number of devices operating together. Moreover, seeking the regulatory analysis process for the IoT devices with technology-specific issues is challenging.

3. *Automation*: To deal with bulk data collection and processing, automation technologies are being widely used to help administrators to enforce specific rules, and to detect anomalous behavior on the networks. However, autonomous systems have their own drawbacks [28]. For instance, a single error in the code or poorly designed algorithm can lead to an entire infrastructure shutting down. Keeping IoT devices secure against attacks and ensuring the protection of the user's data from theft becomes significant in an autonomous environment.

4. *Intelligent Analytics*: IoT applications associated with the extraction of insights from the data depend on analytics that are driven by cognitive technologies. However, there are a number of challenges surrounding these technologies. Flaws in data or the underlying models can lead to inaccurate analysis. In addition, legacy systems are capable of analyzing structured data, however, IoT business interactions are not bound to the generation of structured data only.

4.7 SUMMARY

Challenges in the IoT have a profound impact on its widespread adoption across various areas, while at the same time provide opportunity to the enterprises to find appropriate solutions for the challenges for its future growth. In this chapter, we discussed the different challenges associated with the domain and their effect on the ongoing progress of the field.

In the next chapter, we will discuss the issue of data explosion in the IoT and the existing countermeasures for the data explosion in detail.

REFERENCES

1. Stergiou, C., Psannis, K. E., Gupta, B. B., & Ishibashi, Y. (2018). Security, privacy & efficiency of sustainable cloud computing for big data & IoT. *Sustainable Computing: Informatics and Systems, 19*, 174–184.
2. Tewari, A., & Gupta, B. B. (2018). Security, privacy and trust of different layers in Internet-of-Things (IoTs) framework. *Future Generation Computer Systems.* https://doi.org/10.1016/j.future.2018.04.027.
3. Gupta, B. B., & Sheng, Q. Z. (Eds.). (2019). *Machine learning for computer and cyber security: Principle, algorithms, and practices.* Boca Raton, FL: CRC Press.
4. Gupta, B. B., & Quamara, M. (2018). An overview of Internet of Things (IoT): Architectural aspects, challenges, and protocols. *Concurrency and Computation: Practice and Experience*, e4946.
5. Gupta, B. B., & Agrawal, D. P. (Eds.). (2019). *Handbook of research on cloud computing and big data applications in IoT.* Hershey, PA: IGI Global.
6. Adat, V., & Gupta, B. B. (2018). Security in Internet of Things: Issues, challenges, taxonomy, and architecture. *Telecommunication Systems, 67*(3), 423–441.
7. Plageras, A. P., Stergiou, C., Kokkonis, G., Psannis, K. E., Ishibashi, Y., Kim, B. G., & Gupta, B. B. (2017, July). Efficient large-scale medical data (ehealth big data) analytics in Internet of things. In *2017 IEEE 19th conference on business informatics (CBI)* (Vol. 2, pp. 21–27). IEEE.
8. Fortino, G., Savaglio, C., Palau, C. E., de Puga, J. S., Ganzha, M., Paprzycki, M.,... & Llop, M. (2018). Towards multi-layer interoperability of heterogeneous IoT platforms: The INTER-IoT approach. In *Integration, interconnection, and interoperability of IoT systems* (pp. 199–232). Cham, Switzerland: Springer.
9. Chen, S., Xu, H., Liu, D., Hu, B., & Wang, H. (2014). A vision of IoT: Applications, challenges, and opportunities with china perspective. *IEEE Internet of Things Journal, 1*(4), 349–359.
10. Kanuparthi, A., Karri, R., & Addepalli, S. (2013, November). Hardware and embedded security in the context of internet of things. In *Proceedings of the 2013 ACM workshop on security, privacy & dependability for cyber vehicles* (pp. 61–64). ACM.
11. Taivalsaari, A., & Mikkonen, T. (2017). A roadmap to the programmable world: Software challenges in the IoT era. *IEEE Software, 34*(1), 72–80.
12. Zhang, Z. K., Cho, M. C. Y., Wang, C. W., Hsu, C. W., Chen, C. K., & Shieh, S. (2014, November). IoT security: Ongoing challenges and research opportunities. In *2014 IEEE 7th international conference on service-oriented computing and applications* (pp. 230–234). IEEE.
13. Christin, D., Reinhardt, A., Mogre, P. S., & Steinmetz, R. (2009). Wireless sensor networks and the internet of things: Selected challenges. *Proceedings of the 8th GI/ITG KuVS Fachgespräch Drahtlose sensornetze* (pp. 31–34).

14. Botta, A., De Donato, W., Persico, V., & Pescapé, A. (2014, August). On the integration of cloud computing and Internet of things. In *2014 international conference on future Internet of Things and cloud* (pp. 23–30). IEEE.
15. Mahmoud, R., Yousuf, T., Aloul, F., & Zualkernan, I. (2015, December). Internet of things (IoT) security: Current status, challenges and prospective measures. In *2015 10th international conference for Internet Technology and secured transactions (ICITST)* (pp. 336–341). IEEE.
16. Gupta, B. B., Gupta, S., & Chaudhary, P. (2017). Enhancing the browser-side context-aware sanitization of suspicious HTML5 code for halting the DOM-based XSS vulnerabilities in cloud. *International Journal of Cloud Applications and Computing (IJCAC)*, 7(1), 1–31.
17. Gupta, S., & Gupta, B. B. (2015, May). PHP-sensor: A prototype method to discover workflow violation and XSS vulnerabilities in PHP web applications. In *Proceedings of the 12th ACM international conference on computing frontiers* (p. 59). ACM.
18. Gupta, S., & Gupta, B. B. (2015). BDS: Browser dependent XSS sanitizer. In *Handbook of research on securing cloud-based databases with biometric applications* (pp. 174–191). Hershey, PA: IGI Global.
19. Gupta, S., & Gupta, B. B. (2016). JS-SAN: Defense mechanism for HTML5-based web applications against JavaScript code injection vulnerabilities. *Security and Communication Networks*, 9(11), 1477–1495.
20. Weber, R. H. (2010). Internet of Things–New security and privacy challenges. *Computer Law & Security Review*, 26(1), 23–30.
21. Abera, T., Asokan, N., Davi, L., Koushanfar, F., Paverd, A., Sadeghi, A. R., & Tsudik, G. (2016, June). Things, trouble, trust: On building trust in IoT systems. In *Proceedings of the 53rd annual design automation conference* (p. 121). ACM.
22. Banafa, A. (2017). Three major challenges facing IoT. *IEEE IoT Newsletter*.
23. Samuel, S. S. I. (2016, March). A review of connectivity challenges in IoT-smart home. In *2016 3rd MEC international conference on big data and smart city (ICBDSC)* (pp. 1–4). IEEE.
24. Brass, I., Tanczer, L., Carr, M., & Blackstock, J. (2017). Regulating IoT: Enabling or disabling the capacity of the Internet of Things? *Risk & Regulation*, 33, 12–15.
25. Ren, J., Guo, H., Xu, C., & Zhang, Y. (2017). Serving at the edge: A scalable IoT architecture based on transparent computing. *IEEE Network*, 31(5), 96–105.
26. Sheng, Z., Yang, S., Yu, Y., Vasilakos, A. V., McCann, J. A., & Leung, K. K. (2013). A survey on the IETF protocol suite for the Internet of Things: Standards, challenges, and opportunities. *IEEE Wireless Communications*, 20(6), 91–98.
27. Reyna, A., Martín, C., Chen, J., Soler, E., & Díaz, M. (2018). On blockchain and its integration with IoT. Challenges and opportunities. *Future Generation Computer Systems*, 88, 173–190.
28. Breivold, H. P., & Sandström, K. (2015, December). Internet of things for industrial automation--challenges and technical solutions. In *2015 IEEE International Conference on Data Science and Data Intensive Systems* (pp. 532–539). IEEE.

Data Explosion in IoT

5

5.1 INTRODUCTION

A rapid increase in the data being produced and communicated over IoT networks is observed with 20 quintillions of data being produced every day that include structured, semi-structured, and unstructured textual data, and multimedia content including audio, videos, and images [1,2]. Data associated with physical observations and measurements are among the rapidly growing ones that are generated by the sensor devices with low cost. It is still an unanswered question whether the present IoT systems are efficient enough to handle this data in a meaningful way in terms of storage, processing, and security. To master IoT systems, an understanding of the underlying data model along with the nature of traditional data are necessary. It is also crucial to identify the underlying factors leading to a bulk of data generation. Moreover, the data need to be stored, processed, transmitted, and protected in the right manner [3–6]. In the next section, we discuss the fundamental aspects of big data in the IoT.

5.2 BIG DATA DEFINITION

There is no crisp definition for big data, and moreover, it is not just associated with the size of data. It is typically described based on five key attributes that are also known as the 5Vs – volume, variety, velocity, variability, and value [7]. Volume is related to the size of the data, variety is related to the type and source of the data, velocity is related to the frequency of data generation, variability is related to the changes associated with the structure and semantics of data, and value is related to the advantages of big data to the businesses. These are summarized in Table 5.1.

TABLE 5.1   Big data attributes

ATTRIBUTE	DEFINED BY	DEFINED BY
Volume	Size of data	Terabytes, Petabytes, or Zettabytes
Variety	Type and source of data	Sensors, Physical devices, Social networks, The web, Mobile phones
Velocity	Frequency of generation of data	Every millisecond, Second, Minute, Hour, Day, Week, Month, or Year
Variability	Changes with structure and semantics of data	Anomalies, Inconsistencies
Value	Advantages of data to businesses	Cost cutting, Decision-making, New products and services, Reputation

5.3 UNDERLYING FACTORS FOR DATA EXPLOSION IN THE IoT

In the IoT environment, the amount of data collected and generated will be significantly larger than the past. For instance, the wearable technology including Google Fit, Google Glass, Apple Watch, etc., collect the user's personal and sensitive information associated with their health condition, financial situation, and so forth, from their daily life activities [8,9]. In order to lead in the marketplace, companies (manufacturing, service providers, etc.) have to gain the consumer's confidence and trust, and that can be done through the integration of different technologies. However, the convergence of various technologies is one of the key factors in the massive increase in the data generation in the IoT. These include the following:

1. *Cloud Computing*: Cloud computing has been evolving for a long time, and it has led to the development of mature platforms and IT infrastructure that provide efficient remote solutions. The most commonly known models include Software-as-a-Service, Platform-as-a-Service, and Infrastructure-as-a-Service. On top of them, there are other models including Function-as-a-Service, Desktop-as-a-Service, Database-as-a-Service, and so forth [10–14]. Public cloud models involve exposure of the components and capabilities to the public, whereas private cloud models facilitate the creation of virtual private networks. In addition, hybrid solutions also exist that exploit the benefits of the two.

2. *Data Analytics*: In the last decade, a significant change has been observed in the ways of performing data analytics [15]. Data are approached to get insights at fine-grained levels through advanced technologies that can absorb and store a bulk of data generated by IoT devices. Open source platforms and frameworks along with real-time processing facilities support quick data exploration.

3. *Electronics*: Cheap technologies and faster growth in networks are other factors that foster the generation of a bulk of data. Inexpensive IoT devices and sensors along with more dedicated networks (Narrowband IoT, LoRa, SigFox) are capable of capturing new types of IoT data [16].

5.4 KEY CHALLENGES ASSOCIATED WITH MANAGING THE DATA EXPLOSION IN THE IoT

Some of the key challenges associated with handling the data explosion in the IoT are outlined as follows [17]:

1. *Data Privacy*: The data obtained from a single device may not provide sufficient information, however, the data aggregated from a number of physical devices may foster in creating knowledge of significant importance that can be used in a variety of application areas [18,19]. Various objectives are associated with the data collection and analysis, for instance, improving the user's experience, making strategic decisions, future planning, and so forth. However, these data may be of a sensitive nature and are required to be managed carefully in order to prevent any violations associated with the privacy of data. Addressing privacy thus becomes an important concern, and it becomes the responsibility of various stakeholders associated with the development and use of technology to ensure privacy-preserving ecosystem.

2. *Data Ownership*: In the IoT era, data owners must be provided with full control over their data, and they must be able to choose what operations service providers can perform over the data [20]. However, with limited user access, it becomes challenging.

3. *Customization*: Users must be given the privilege to choose underlying components (hardware or software) from various vendors for creating their smart environment [21]. In addition, they must be

provided with the freedom of choosing or withdrawing the required services from different service providers. However, facilitating this becomes difficult because of the lack of transparency in the actions of the vendors or service providers, as they can disable some features or remove some capabilities without the user's knowledge.

4. *Knowledge Extraction*: IoT solutions provide functionalities based on raw data collection and analysis [22]. However, with the advent of new technologies, businesses may derive more knowledge from the user-specific data and may use the data for making revenues, and, in some cases, the data can be misused. In such scenarios, users must be informed about the future possibilities and possible consequences of the data collected from them.

5. *Anonymity*: Data communication in networks may involve tracing the communication paths with some parameters [23]. It can be used by the data analytics to obtain knowledge through fingerprinting and profile generation. Hence, the location of the user can be tracked. In response to this, new technologies must be discovered in order to perform anonymization of the communication path for ensuring data privacy.

6. *Data Integration*: Data integration is one of biggest hurdles experienced by businesses in the adoption of the IoT [24]. Integrating enormous volumes of data collected from different sources while maintaining the precision is complex. The continuous increase in the number of inter-connected devices that are engaged in gathering data from the network edge makes it difficult to keep track of the data flow. In addition, these data may be accompanied with noise and redundant information that makes them even hard to use.

7. *Data Management*: There is not enough storage currently to meet the storage demands of the data to be generated by IoT devices in the future [25]. Developing a data management framework involves making decisions on the nature of data to be stored and ways to access them for analysis, which is a major challenge or decision for the enterprises.

5.5 TECHNOLOGICAL SUPPORT

Different technological paradigms play crucial roles in dealing with the issue of the data explosion in the IoT. In the following subsections, we discuss some of the commonly used paradigms [17,26].

5.5.1 Machine Learning

Upon capturing the data from IoT devices and sensors, communication protocols are used for dumping the information to a sink. Afterwards, data mediation and processing are done, and aggregation is performed. During this process, machine learning is applied that enables the following:

1. *Anomaly Detection*: It involves identification of the anomalies in IoT data streams coming from the sensing devices.
2. *Predictive Modeling*: It involves making predictions using historical data.
3. *Data Classification*: It involves grouping the data into different categories.

A standard methodology is followed to apply machine-learning solutions on big data in the IoT. It involves understanding the business, its goals, and the analytic approach in order to obtain the desired outcome. Afterwards, data collection is done, which is then validated. Once the understanding is built, the data are prepared, after which a model is developed. This model is then evaluated with respect to different parameters, for instance, accuracy, and finally deployed. Adjustments to the model are made upon getting the feedback.

5.5.2 Artificial Intelligence

Artificial intelligence is another discipline, the development and use of which is now beginning [27]. Artificial intelligence is getting attention with respect to the IoT, and in the coming few years, it is expected to be turned into a significant investment for many enterprises. Artificial intelligence has the capability to gather, contextualize, understand, and act on a bulk of data, thus giving rise to a new category of applications. These applications have the capability to adapt to continuously changing conditions. The more data that are available for analysis, the better the quality of the outcome will be.

5.5.3 Intelligent Edge Processing

As the sensors collecting data are approaching billions of inter-connected things, enterprises require a way for cleaning and filtering the bulk of data. Intelligent edge processing is one such solution that facilitates the creation of value near to the source of data generation, i.e., edge, through following differentiators [28]:

1. *Presence*: New algorithms, architectures, frameworks, and customized data technology enable enterprises to perform local data processing. Data processing is done where it is created and where it is consumed, thereby preventing the requirement of transmitting data to remote servers in order to reduce the corresponding cost.

2. *Performance*: Intelligent edge processing enhances business performance by providing better data management and identifying the relevancy of data to be stored along with event detection. With the combination of operational technology with IT, complex events can be processed in batches that improve performance with respect to speed and quality.

3. *Power*: Intelligent edge computing enables process execution without causing delays in transferring data to the cloud.

4. *Protection*: Intelligent edge processing ensures the required level of security in the case of IoT implementations. These implementations promote openness and are designed in such a way that these are compatible to work with other networks. It facilitates unique identification of sensors, data encryption, and validation checks on the data. Such an on-site processing is required in order to avoid the latency caused in sending data to the cloud, which can also open loopholes to be exploited by the attackers.

5.6 SUMMARY

In this chapter, we discussed the underlying factors behind the data explosion in the IoT along with associated key challenges and roles of some of the technological paradigms in handling the data explosion. In the next chapter, we will discuss the concept of autonomous driving vehicles as an application area of the IoT.

REFERENCES

1. IBM. http://www-01.ibm.com/software/data/bigdata. Accessed May 2019.
2. Barnaghi, P., Sheth, A., & Henson, C. (2013). From data to actionable knowledge: Big data challenges in the web of things. *IEEE Intelligent Systems*, 28(6), 6–11.

3. Stergiou, C., Psannis, K. E., Gupta, B. B., & Ishibashi, Y. (2018). Security, privacy & efficiency of sustainable cloud computing for big data & IoT. *Sustainable Computing: Informatics and Systems*, *19*, 174–184.

4. Tewari, A., & Gupta, B. B. (2018). Security, privacy and trust of different layers in Internet-of-Things (IoTs) framework. *Future Generation Computer Systems*. https://doi.org/10.1016/j.future.2018.04.027.

5. Gupta, B. B., & Sheng, Q. Z. (Eds.). (2019). *Machine learning for computer and cyber security: Principle, algorithms, and practices*. Boca Raton, FL: CRC Press.

6. Gupta, B. B., & Agrawal, D. P. (Eds.). (2019). *Handbook of research on cloud computing and big data applications in IoT*. Hershey, PA: IGI Global.

7. Addo-Tenkorang, R., & Helo, P. T. (2016). Big data applications in operations/supply-chain management: A literature review. *Computers & Industrial Engineering*, *101*, 528–543.

8. Adat, V., & Gupta, B. B. (2018). Security in Internet of Things: Issues, challenges, taxonomy, and architecture. *Telecommunication Systems*, *67*(3), 423–441.

9. Plageras, A. P., Stergiou, C., Kokkonis, G., Psannis, K. E., Ishibashi, Y., Kim, B. G., & Gupta, B. B. (2017, July). Efficient large-scale medical data (ehealth big data) analytics in Internet of things. In *2017 IEEE 19th conference on business informatics (CBI)* (Vol. 2, pp. 21–27). IEEE.

10. Hashem, I. A. T., Yaqoob, I., Anuar, N. B., Mokhtar, S., Gani, A., & Khan, S. U. (2015). The rise of "big data" on cloud computing: Review and open research issues. *Information Systems*, *47*, 98–115.

11. Gupta, B. B., Gupta, S., & Chaudhary, P. (2017). Enhancing the browser-side context-aware sanitization of suspicious HTML5 code for halting the DOM-based XSS vulnerabilities in cloud. *International Journal of Cloud Applications and Computing (IJCAC)*, *7*(1), 1–31.

12. Gou, Z., Yamaguchi, S., & Gupta, B. B. (2017). Analysis of various security issues and challenges in cloud computing environment: A survey. In *Identity theft: Breakthroughs in research and practice* (pp. 221–247). Hershey, PA: IGI Global.

13. Gupta, B. B., Yamaguchi, S., & Agrawal, D. P. (2018). Advances in security and privacy of multimedia big data in mobile and cloud computing. *Multimedia Tools and Applications*, *77*(7), 9203–9208.

14. Gupta, B. B., & Badve, O. P. (2017). Taxonomy of DoS and DDoS attacks and desirable defense mechanism in a cloud computing environment. *Neural Computing and Applications*, *28*(12), 3655–3682.

15. Chen, H., Chiang, R. H., & Storey, V. C. (2012). Business intelligence and analytics: From big data to big impact. *MIS Quarterly*, *36*(4), 1165–1188.

16. Sadler, J. M., Ames, D. P., & Khattar, R. (2016). A recipe for standards-based data sharing using open source software and low-cost electronics. *Journal of Hydroinformatics*, *18*(2), 185–197.

17. Talend. https://www.talend.com/resources/iot-data/. Accessed May 2019.

18. Perera, C., Ranjan, R., Wang, L., Khan, S. U., & Zomaya, A. Y. (2015). Big data privacy in the Internet of things era. *IT Professional*, *17*(3), 32–39.

19. Patil, H. K., & Seshadri, R. (2014, June). Big data security and privacy issues in healthcare. In *2014 IEEE international congress on big data* (pp. 762–765). IEEE.

20. Mashhadi, A., Kawsar, F., & Acer, U. G. (2014, March). Human data interaction in IoT: The ownership aspect. In *2014 IEEE world forum on Internet of Things (WF-IoT)* (pp. 159–162). IEEE.

21. Bodin, W., Jaramillo, D., Redman, J., & Thorson, D. (2007). Method for data management and data rendering for disparate data types. U.S. Patent Application No. 11/226,744.

22. Bin, S., Yuan, L., & Xiaoyi, W. (2010, April). Research on data mining models for the Internet of things. In *2010 international conference on image analysis and signal processing* (pp. 127–132). IEEE.

23. Guan, Z., Zhang, Y., Wu, L., Wu, J., Li, J., Ma, Y., & Hu, J. (2019). APPA: An anonymous and privacy preserving data aggregation scheme for fog-enhanced IoT. *Journal of Network and Computer Applications, 125,* 82–92.

24. Tonyali, S., Akkaya, K., Saputro, N., Uluagac, A. S., & Nojoumian, M. (2018). Privacy-preserving protocols for secure and reliable data aggregation in IoT-enabled smart metering systems. *Future Generation Computer Systems, 78,* 547–557.

25. Ma, M., Wang, P., & Chu, C. H. (2013, August). Data management for Internet of things: Challenges, approaches and opportunities. In *2013 IEEE international conference on green computing and communications and IEEE Internet of Things and IEEE cyber, physical and social computing* (pp. 1144–1151). IEEE.

26. Al-Jarrah, O. Y., Yoo, P. D., Muhaidat, S., Karagiannidis, G. K., & Taha, K. (2015). Efficient machine learning for big data: A review. *Big Data Research,* 2(3), 87–93.

27. O'Leary, D. E. (2013). Artificial intelligence and big data. *IEEE Intelligent Systems, 28*(2), 96–99.

28. Cdlbiz. https://www.cdlbiz.com/uploads/5/0/1/6/50168079/sap_whitepaper_edge.pdf. Accessed May 2019.

Computing Paradigms and Security Issues in Connected and Autonomous Driving Vehicles

6

6.1 INTRODUCTION

In the previous few years, a noteworthy increase in the degree of inter-connectivity among vehicles and automation has been witnessed by the field of transportation systems. Connectivity enables the establishment of communication among vehicles and core infrastructure for transmitting the information related to the vehicle's current location, speed, control parameters, and so forth (Figure 6.1). Automation includes monitoring the environmental conditions using sensor technology and using the collected information along with some already determined knowledge for planning the vehicle's activity. The enormous development of connected and autonomous driving vehicles (CADVs), also known as smart vehicles, is driven by the evolving underlying technologies and desire to bring driverless, comfortable, safer, resilient, and more responsive vehicles with robust transport infrastructure to the market. Traffic mobility, efficient energy consumption, and environmental protection

FIGURE 6.1 Capabilities of autonomous vehicles.

from pollution are key promoting aspects for the increasing demand of these smart vehicles. According to the predictions made by the Institute of Electrical and Electronics Engineers, 75% of the vehicles across the world will become autonomous by 2040 [1].

However, similar to other computing systems and networks, human-centric smart vehicles and the inter-connected transport infrastructure are also vulnerable to potential security risks with an increasing likelihood of attacks in the future [2]. These attacks can be common security attacks and vicious attacks. The former includes breach of location privacy of the person, distributed denial of service (DDoS) attacks against the core transport infrastructure and utilities, integrity attacks over the valuable information collected from the nearby vehicles, etc. The latter includes disabling the breaks of the vehicle and the malfunctioning of the other control aspects of the system. Due to the absence of standby driving control or the driver being busy in background activities, these attacks may lead to disastrous results.

In spite of the fact that the underlying computing technologies have become successful in bringing CADVs to the market en masse, the vulnerabilities related to them have a direct or indirect impact over the acceptance trend of these vehicles, which in turn becomes a hurdle for policymakers and developers. In this regard, the current chapter discusses the underlying technologies and computing paradigms involved in the development of autonomous vehicles. A substantial work effort is invested in identifying the existing security and privacy issues, along with the potential solutions to mitigate them [3–8].

6.2 CONNECTED AND AUTONOMOUS DRIVING VEHICLE – A TECHNICAL BACKGROUND

CADVs are unmanned self-governing vehicles that are configured in a manner for supporting autonomous driving through communication with the devices external to the vehicles. Autonomous driving involves recognizing or sensing the surroundings and adaptive navigation with minimal or no human intervention. Figure 6.2 shows the levels of automation for road vehicles as defined by Society of Automotive Engineers [9]. These are based on the underlying controlling functions, nature of involvement of human driver, and performance of the vehicle.

6.2.1 Functional Blocks

A typical CADV is comprised of various functional blocks categorized into generalized blocks and specific blocks that receive input from outside, process it, and produce the output [10]. Generalized blocks, also known as high-level blocks, such as sensors and environmental maps (capture 3D appearance of the surroundings), are more general toward different applications. On the other

SAE Autonomy Level	•Control •Additional Support
Level 0 - No Automation	• Fully human-driven vehicles • Enhancement through warning and intervention systems
Level 1 - Driver Assistance	• Automated system controls the vehicle's steering or acceleration/declaration • Remaining aspects are performed by the human driver
Level 2 - Partial Automation	• Automated system controls the vehicle's steering and acceleration/declaration • Remaining aspects are performed by the human driver
Level 3 - Conditional Automation	• Dynamic driving tasks under automated system's control • Human intervention required when asked for
Level 4 - High Automation	• Dynamic driving tasks under automated system's control • Human intervention not required
Level 5 - Full Automation	• Self-driving vehicles • All driving modes under system's control

FIGURE 6.2   Society of Automotive Engineers (SAE) – levels of automation.

hand, specific blocks or low-level blocks, such as global positioning systems (GPS) and road network maps (capture information about road network and path markings), are designed in order to perform application-specific functions. Core infrastructure that includes Roadside Units, traffic signals, streetlights, parking meters, cameras, and map servers maintains the vehicle-specific information and other environmental parameters. The external communication module is responsible for the transmission of the information from the vehicles to the core infrastructure, other vehicles, or remote cloud server. The inter-connection among these functional blocks is depicted by Figure 6.3. The working of autonomous vehicles involves the sensing of information, processing of information, planning of the future actions, and taking the control actions. The overall communication between different entities can be grouped into the following [11,12]:

- *Vehicle-to-Vehicle Communication*: It enables vehicles to share the collected information among them. This information typically includes information related to local traffic, congestion, road conditions, accidents, parking availability, and so forth.
- *Vehicle-to-Infrastructure Communication*: It enables interaction between the vehicles and the core infrastructure to share information in order to optimize the use of the road network to reduce congestion, environmental pollution, and so forth. This type of communication is wireless and involves a bi-directional flow of information.
- *Vehicle-to-Cloud Communication*: It enables vehicles to communicate with remote cloud servers in order to exchange information that is stored for the long term and is used by the vehicles in order

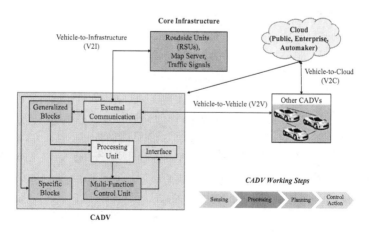

FIGURE 6.3   Inter-connection among CADV modules.

to serve a particular purpose. This type of communication is also used for providing collaborative services including entertainment, e-Health, and so forth.

Apart from the above discussed communication categories, Vehicle-to-Pedestrian (through devices, such as smartphones) [13] and Vehicle-to-Network [14] communication terminologies are also becoming popular. Vehicle-to-Everything communication refers to the transmission of information collected by the embedded vehicular sensors to other entities that are directly or indirectly associated with the vehicles [15].

The following subsections discuss the technologies involved in the development and functioning of CADVs and some of their positive aspects, along with some forecasts associated with CADVs.

6.2.2 Underlying Technologies

6.2.2.1 Radio Detection and Ranging

Automated vehicles are equipped with radio detection and ranging (RADAR) that emits radio waves. When these radio waves fall on an object, bounce off, and return back to the receiver, that helps in estimating the distance from the object. Short range radars are capable of detecting the distance from objects up to 20 meters away, medium range radars have the capability to look for objects up to 80 meters away, and long range radars can detect objects up to 150 meters away. Short range radar utilizes cameras to provide information about angles, while long range radar provides directional information. Short range radars are used in collision warning, blind spot warning, and parking assistance. On the other hand, long range radars are used in automatic cruise control (ACC) for determining the distance from the vehicle in front as well as the speed of the vehicle and in automatic emergency braking systems. Metallic objects at RADAR frequencies reflect a signal at significant levels, while non-metallic objects including rainwater and rocks do not, which makes them invisible at radio frequencies [16].

Gong et al. [17] presented a cooperative ACC design for CADVs considering topological structure for dynamic flow of information and compared the ACC design with fixed information flow topological structure. Branson [18] proposed a system for RADAR localization in CADVs.

6.2.2.2 Light Detection and Ranging

Light detection and ranging (LiDAR) is a surveying technology that involves the emission of laser signals that bounce back from the object for calculating its distance from the vehicle based on the time the signal takes to travel the complete distance. It can also determine angles accurately in horizontal and vertical directions and generates 3D data having an accuracy lying within 2 centimeters. These data when integrated with 2D map data allow automatic navigation by vehicles. It is used for trajectory planning and aerial survey to produce high-resolution maps for the automated vehicles to work with and for obstacle avoidance. These have a wider field of view, enabling the detection of obstacles over the curves. Since LiDAR utilizes a relatively shorter wavelength than RADAR from the electromagnetic spectrum that makes it suitable to map an obstacle of the same size or larger than the wavelength, it produces more accurate mapping in comparison to RADAR systems. LiDAR measurements can be fused with RADAR and a color camera for grid-based processing and detection and tracking of multiple objects.

Gao et al. [19] proposed a method for object classification using a Convolutional Neural Network-based fusion of vision and LiDAR data. Chesworth et al. [20] discussed the optical requirements for LiDAR-based transmitter systems for autonomous vehicles. Gleaves et al. [21] discussed an advanced millimeter wave all-weather RADAR with a long range and high resolution. This RADAR enables multiple targets detection using monopulse signal processing, electronic scanning, and IQ mixing. Zofka et al. [22] proposed a framework called Sleepwalker, for verification and validation of CADVs using LiDAR simulations.

6.2.2.3 Global Positioning System

Satellite technology is utilized by a GPS to provide position- or location-specific information within a range of 5 meters. A GPS is affected by a number of factors including the presence of tunnels, radio interference, weather conditions, and urban canyons [23]. To obtain better coverage, an increased number of satellites are used. To locate the vehicle and for establishing its initial position, the GPS receiver takes between 30 to 60 seconds. Hence, the vehicle has to delay its departure in order to get this initial fix computed. A GPS in the public domain has open access, whereas in military applications, it uses encrypted signals to transmit the information.

Liu et al. [24] proposed a GPS navigation algorithm based on an adaptive Kalman filter considering the information fusion method. The method is capable of determining the noise value and suppressing the white noise.

6.2.2.4 Ultrasonic Sensors

Ultrasonic sensors use high-frequency sound waves for measuring the time of flight of the reflected sound in order to determine the distance from the object [25]. If l denotes the distance of the object from the vehicle, v denotes the speed of ultrasonic waves in the air, t denotes the time of flight, and a denotes the angle of the path taken by the waves with the horizontal direction, then using following relation, l can be determined as [26]:

$$l = \frac{vt \cos a}{2}.$$

The concept of Doppler shift can be used for moving object. These sensors are used while lane keeping, reversing, parking, and ACC.

Li et al. [27] presented an approach for obstacle tracking using ultrasonic sensors arranged in a linear fashion. The authors compared their performance with the triangle positioning method.

6.2.2.5 Dedicated Short Range Communications

Dedicated short range communications is a one- or two-way wireless communication protocol for enabling short-to-medium range communication among automated vehicles and between vehicle and stationary transport infrastructure. This protocol is appropriate for enhancing the safety system for navigation, infotainment, and collision warning. Sensing is enabled that is not just restricted to line-of-sight, i.e., for alert generation in case of objects that cannot be seen directly.

Wang et al. [28] proposed a collision warning method based on information fusion of dedicated short range communications and GPS, and using an adaptive Kalman filter to predict the trajectory of the vehicle and for analyzing the collision probability.

6.2.2.6 Cameras

Cameras are used for the recognition of lane markings over the road and road signs through the detection of boundaries and color. These can be used for the measurement of rate of change between the objects in the front, such as whether the driver is overtaking a relatively slower moving vehicle or a pedestrian. Unlike other sensors, cameras can also be used to obtain the geography related information. These are used for the object recognition and detection of obstacles. Fusion with other sensors can be utilized to obtain the 360-degree information. Based on the number of cameras in use, autonomous vehicles can act as mono-vision systems in which along with the camera, different sensors are used to determine information about other aspects (such as depth), and stereo systems are used in which the overlapping area of two cameras is used to determine the depth.

Elie et al. [29] devised a system for autonomous valet parking by utilizing plenoptic cameras. Cao et al. [30] presented a navigation framework using stereo cameras for autonomous vehicles and compared the performance with a conventional Cartesian-based method.

6.2.2.7 Other Sensors

Inertial Measurement Units including accelerometers, gyroscopes, and inclination sensors are used to provide acceleration, velocity, and orientation information. Park et al. [31] proposed a lateral control system for lane keeping in CADVs involving the collection of directional data by Inertial Measurement Unit sensors and vision sensors. Tire-pressure monitor systems are used to provide tire-specific information, such as number of rotations in a given time that can be utilized to determine the radius of the wheel. Engine control sensors are used to provide engine-related information including temperature, air flow, and exhaust gas that is utilized for regulating engine activity or to adjust engine conditions [32]. The functionality of the vehicle is controlled through acquisition, processing, and electronic signals.

6.2.2.8 Mapping Technologies

Mapping technologies are used to map the roads with higher resolution with the use of variables. These maps contain information related to the lane markings, slope and width of road, and so forth. Digital maps are not restricted to line-of-sight and have relatively greater range than conventional sensors. Bosch, Google, and Nokia are some of the leading industries that have developed their own navigation systems for environmental map generation [33–35].

Maturana et al. [36] described a navigation system based on semantic mapping and geometric coding for off-road driving. Li et al. [37] presented a collaborative mapping-based autonomous parking system for multi-story parking using Bayesian probabilistic updating and 3D LiDAR point cloud registration.

6.2.2.9 Route Planning and Navigation Algorithms

Route planning algorithms aim at determining the shortest route toward a destination. In case of blocked regions and high traffic, they are responsible for determining the alternate and faster routes. These algorithms consider exits, road intersections, and on-ramps as decision points, whereas links are taken as the roads connecting them. Environmental information is also used for planning a lane change or taking a smooth turn. After route planning is done, navigation algorithms are utilized so that the vehicle is able to navigate through the selected routes. Particle swarm optimization [38], fuzzy logic [39], deep learning [40], and machine learning [41] are some of the popular concepts for developing route-planning algorithms.

González et al. [42] presented a review of different motion planning algorithms for intelligent vehicles. Zhang et al. [43] proposed a steering control approach for path tracking using fuzzy modeling considering parametric uncertainties. Schambers et al. [44] proposed a route-planning algorithm for CADVs using the Bellman-Ford algorithm and implemented the algorithm on an embedded Graphical Processing Unit system.

6.2.3 Potential Benefits and Forecasts

Since the way operations are performed by CADVs is essentially different from human-driven vehicles, these can be programmed in a manner to optimize their functionality in order to deliver maximum benefits. Following are some of the expected key advantages of CADVs [45,46]:

- *Unmanned Vehicles*: People with disability or older citizens will also be able to garner the benefits of autonomous vehicles. There will be no need to get a driving license or to undergo a driving test.
- *Efficient Transportation*: Reduced congestion, increase in lane capacity, and real-time route optimization are some of the factors that would lead to efficient transportation. Autonomous vehicles will make the traffic flow efficient by avoiding traffic congestion. Real-time information will be used for route determination and optimization through communication among the vehicles and the core infrastructure. These are designed in a way to optimize efficiency of the control system including braking and acceleration, which in turn would cause lesser fuel consumption, thereby improving the fuel efficiency.
- *Safety*: From the safety point-of-view, autonomous vehicles will drastically reduce the occurrence of accidents because of the decrease in the rate of human control and minimum involvement of human errors. Factors like slow reaction time, lack of experience, overspeeding, and distracted driving that are some of the main causes of road accidents will be omitted while autonomous vehicles in use.
- *Robust and Resilient Transport Infrastructure*: Core infrastructure will be able to maintain an acceptable level of performance even in the case of internal and external disturbances, such as malicious and unexpected threats.
- *Environmentally friendly Vehicles*: Reduced fuel and energy consumption will certainly reduce the emissions from the autonomous vehicles. Fuel consumption increases while driving at high speeds, while applying brakes, and during re-acceleration. The driving style of autonomous vehicles will cut out these factors, thereby resulting in lesser battery power consumption, burning of fuel, and environmental pollution.

It has been predicted that the market size of partially autonomous vehicles will reach 36 billion U.S. dollars, and the market size for fully autonomous vehicles will reach 6 billion U.S. dollars by the year 2025 [47]. As per the claims of optimists, 90% of the contribution in crashes comes from the human errors, and consequently, autonomous vehicles will reduce the contribution by 90% [48]. The world's leading automakers including Ford, BMW, Honda, Toyota, Renault, Nissan, and Volvo are planning and investing to bring autonomous cars on the road in the coming decade [49].

6.3 COMPUTING PARADIGMS

The three main computing paradigms for CADVs are depicted in Figure 6.4 and are discussed in the following subsections.

6.3.1 Artificial Intelligence

Intelligent automation or automated driving technology involves embedded decision-making over the processed data or information, which in turn is based on inherent artificial intelligence (AI). Although the simulation of the complete intellectual proficiency of the human brain will take a long time, still it is possible to map some of the cognitive activities of humans to

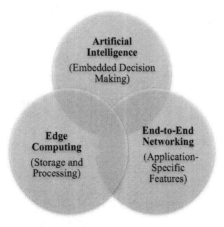

FIGURE 6.4   CADV computing paradigms.

machine intelligence for the formulation of driving cognition. Gartner made a survey according to which, as of mid-2017, more than 46 companies are developing AI-based software for controlling the functionality of autonomous vehicles [50]. AI utilizes audio cognition, visual cognition, concentration, consciousness, thinking, and decision-making capabilities of the human brain. It serves three core functionalities in automated driving – sensing (involves environmental perception and passing the information through highly powerful computational devices to generate an environmental model that includes details about the road, obstacles, and pedestrians), mapping (involves updating the environmental view with the current one in a real-time fashion), and driving policy (embedded into the driving platform through which the vehicle is capable of informing the situation of the surroundings on the basis of which strategy is built and decisions are made) [51]. Sensor information and intelligent decision-making are decoupled in order to prevent the number and position of sensors putting any direct impact on the decision-making.

Artificial vision is deployed in autonomous driving technology to perform the driving tasks including [52]:

* *Detection of Lane*: It involves localization of the road (by creating a map of the appropriate path), determining the approximate or relative position between the road and the vehicle, and analyzing the way or direction in which the vehicle is heading. A number of lane detection approaches exist in the literature, including localization of painted markings on the road surface or lane markings, use of color cameras for unstructured roads, use of concentric circles, focusing on the small area over the road ahead of the vehicle, statistical methods, chromatic saturation, polynomial representation, contour-based methods, linear lane models, triangular road models, and so forth.

* *Detection of Obstacle*: It involves localization of all the possible obstacles on the vehicle's path. These obstacles can be other vehicles or some other generic objects on the road. Obstacle detection techniques include edge detection and obstacle modeling, localization of the vehicles based on the search for specific patterns (such as shape and symmetry), identification of free space, analysis of optical flow (sequence of two or more images), and processing of nonmonocular image sets that involves identification of resemblance or correspondences among pixels in different images (stereo vision and trinocular vision).

* *Detection of Pedestrian*: It involves localization of the pedestrian across the road. It is still a challenging task to detect people because of their different dressing style, scenic background, and sudden

change in background. Approaches for pedestrian detection include pattern analysis, use of stereo vision, shape detection, and tracking. The focus of these approaches is to recognize human shape and gait and segmentation with stereo and motion.

Chen et al. [53] presented a supervised learning-based algorithm using a barrier function for obstacle avoidance in low-speed autonomous vehicles. This algorithm works in integration with a navigation algorithm in a plug-and-play fashion.

6.3.2 Vehicular Cloud Computing or Edge Computing

Environmental conditions are sensed by the sensor platforms, and information related to the road conditions, GPS location, and so on is collected. Vehicles are also getting advanced from simple data consumers to data producers. They utilize embedded sensor technology and generate a bulk of data. The sensed data undergo data filtration and are uploaded over the cloud [54]. However, in some cases, this data cannot be uploaded over the cloud for processing due to security reasons. While dealing with applications that involve a bulk of data requiring real-time processing, edge computing provides an appropriate solution. It involves processing the data closer to their source and utilizes distributed computing infrastructure locally.

For providing the collected data and information to the drivers or vehicles, these intelligent agents or vehicles promote local collaborations through content sharing with a goal of providing a rich user experience. Mobile cloud technology, also known as vehicular cloud, is the core system environment temporarily created for providing the essential services to the autonomous vehicles including content sharing and search, routing, data dissemination, and attack protection. Vehicles within a local relevance with enhanced processing and storage processing capabilities and Roadside Units as a stationary member constitute the cloud within which vehicular services are generated, managed, and consumed. It uses open interfaces and standards to provide autonomous vehicle applications that are shared by manufacturing industries. It enables efficient communication, extends the interaction capability, and provides a distributed processing environment to a network of autonomous vehicles by integrating the sensor technology, data fusion, and database sharing applications.

The typical applications of vehicular cloud computing (VCC) in the autonomous vehicle industry include maintenance of the vehicles using software updates, prevention of traffic congestion, sharing information about road conditions, accident alerts and safety applications, parking management, and evacuation planning [55]. Autonomous vehicles incorporate three categories of inter-linked resources – sensors, computational units, and storage units. Sensors are involved in self-actuation and detecting the physical world events, and external systems read and control these sensors through the Internet. Computational resources perform processing over the sensed data, whereas storage resources store the sensed or processed data and enable data sharing.

Establishment of a virtual vehicular computing platform involves different phases that are discussed as below [56]:

- *Cloud resource discovery or detection*: In this phase, a cloud leader creates a temporary VCC platform for completing an autonomous driving application. It broadcasts a resource request message among vehicles and Roadside Units in the vicinity that can serve with the desired sensing resources, which in turn depends upon the nature of application.
- *Cloud formation*: In this phase, the cloud leader, on receiving the appropriate reply messages containing the resource information from the cloud members, creates a new cloud by selecting these cloud members.
- *Task assignment and result collection*: In this phase, the cloud leader assigns the appropriate tasks to the cloud members in order to fulfill the application requirement and collects the relevant results from them.
- *Content sharing*: In this phase, the cloud leader processes the information collected from the cloud members and broadcasts it across all the nodes in the network. The autonomous vehicles designated for the relevant application consume this information. In addition, other vehicles store the content for future reuse.
- *Maintenance of cloud*: Cloud members may send a message for leaving the cloud to the leader, and the job of the leader is to replace that member with another so that the application requirements can be fulfilled.
- *Cloud release*: The cloud leader sends a cloud release message to all the members once the cloud has served the purpose and is of no use.

6.3.3 End-to-End Networking

End-to-end networking is associated with the application-specific features residing at the end nodes or communication endpoints rather than intermediary nodes, such as routers or gateways. CADV systems are embedded with an obstacle avoidance system that works by mapping the raw input images to possible steering angles [57]. For example, end-to-end neural networks can be trained to take images captured by the camera as input and to steer the vehicle in order to navigate in a parking lot. Supervised learning is used for training these systems in order to predict the steering angles based on the ones provided by the human driver during different training scenarios, such as different weather conditions, lighting conditions, obstacles, and terrain types.

Xu et al. [58] presented a model based on end-to-end learning from crowd-sourced video data for predicting the motion of autonomous vehicles using monocular camera images. Bojarski et al. [59] discussed an end-to-end approach to train a convolutional neural network to map pixels from the single front-facing camera placed in the vehicle into steering commands.

6.4 SECURITY ISSUES AND EXISTING COUNTERMEASURES

With the increasing dependency on the underlying hardware and software platforms to make navigation decisions in CADVs, it becomes equally important to understand the security related risks and barriers. Moreover, it is necessary to figure out the possible solutions and the feasibility of implementing the security [60]. These can be associated with the system software and hardware, applications, communication network, and driver's privacy [61]. Security attacks associated with autonomous vehicles revolve across a number of factors, including attacking agent, attacker agent, motivation toward attack, level of expertise required, system access, system knowledge, and window opportunity as highlighted in Figure 6.5 [10,62,63]. Other than these, the time elapsed for identifying the vulnerabilities, available equipment, and impact of the attacks are some of the promoting factors.

In the following subsections, we cover some of the security challenges and existing countermeasures from the literature that are related to the underlying computing paradigms as well as with the associated entities in CADV systems (Figure 6.6).

6.4.1 Challenges and Countermeasures Associated with Computing Paradigms

Table 6.1 summarizes the security issues and corresponding countermeasures associated with different computing paradigms involved in the development of the autonomous vehicles.

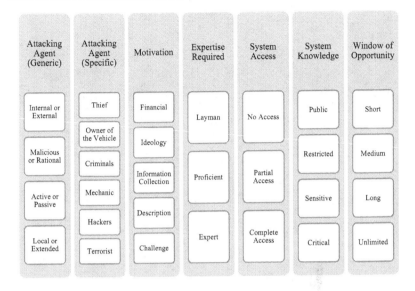

FIGURE 6.5 Factors associated with security attacks against autonomous vehicles.

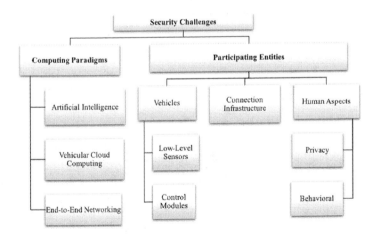

FIGURE 6.6 Taxonomy of security challenges in CADV technology.

TABLE 6.1 Security challenges and existing countermeasures associated with computing paradigms

COMPUTING PARADIGM	SECURITY CHALLENGES	IMPACT	COUNTERMEASURES
AI	Poor design	Unexpected behavior	Safety by design, isolation, and segmentation, software updates
	Bad weather conditions	Uncontrolled behavior	Planning and testing
	Introduction of vulnerabilities through reward hacking	Manipulated working	Trip wires, reward pre-training, adversarial blinding
	Improper coordination	Accidents	Constrained-based learning
	Level of freedom of control and independence	Increasing chances of aggregate failures	Training in risk-free simulated environment
	Changing environmental conditions	Unexpected behavior	Deliberative and reactive planning
VCC	DoS attacks such as jamming	Information unavailability	Frequency hopping, channel switching, use of multiple transceivers, congestion database
	Malware injection	Resource exhaustion	Intrusion Detection System (IDS), system integrity check
	Information disclosure	Privacy breach and information misuse	Data anonymization, multi-factor protection schemes
	Privilege elevation	Unauthorized access to protected data or resources	Authentication, scalable security schemes
End-to-End Networking	Push-based features	Security issues in unreliable network conditions	Partial control distribution (fog nodes)
	Malware	Unexpected behavior	Alert generation mechanisms

6.4.1.1 Artificial Intelligence

Poor structure of AI-based frameworks is responsible for numerous pragmatic security issues. Bad climate conditions can make AI-based smart vehicles behave like uncontrolled machines that can prompt unexpected behavior. Vulnerabilities can be presented in the processing framework so as to control its working, for example, reward hacking [64]. Improper coordination can prompt mishaps. For example, the vehicle can squash anything on the way while searching for the fastest course to arrive at the destination. Another issue is to choose the opportunity of control and autonomy that ought to be given to the AI. Furthermore, structuring a robust AI-based vehicle that can adjust to the progressions through behavioral analysis in various natural conditions is additionally challenging.

To manage security risks related to a poor design issue, developers and manufacturers should concentrate on embracing security mechanisms at each progression of the advancement of the product rather than only focusing on the usefulness of the finished result. Critical framework functionalities must be kept isolated from the non-critical assignments, for example, entertainment, by utilizing isolation and segmentation. System and application programs must be kept up-to-date. Moreover, to manage bad climate conditions, appropriate planning and testing of the vehicle ought to be guaranteed before the shipment. To keep away from the danger of vulnerabilities in the framework, for example, reward hacking, techniques like introduction of trip wires, reward pre-training, and adversarial blinding can be embraced [64]. To manage coordination issues, constrained-based learning systems can be embraced to improve productivity. In order to solve the independence problem, vehicles with AI control must be prepared in hazard-free simulated conditions with unquestionable trials. To make CADV capable enough to adjust to evolving conditions, deliberative planning can be adopted for predictable ecological conditions and responsive planning can be embraced for unpredictable conditions [65].

Lu et al. [66] discussed the impact of taking the images from different distances and angles to prevent the fooling of object detection in CADVs using adversarial examples. George et al. [67] discussed the role of AI in ensuring the security of the communication in CADVs. Siau et al. [68] discussed the concept of trust with respect to AI, machine learning, and robotics, and the factors crucial for the establishment and continuity of trust in AI. Alheeti et al. [69] proposed an intrusion detection system for external communication in CADVs using backpropagation networks to defend against DoS attacks.

6.4.1.2 Vehicular Cloud Computing

Resource sharing in VCC promotes attacks against the cloud platform itself [70,71]. DoS attacks, such as jamming, can be directed so as to avoid the accessibility of the data over the virtual cloud formed by the vehicle for navigation purposes. A hardware security module that is in charge of executing cryptographic operations of the framework is constrained by an upper bound on the maximum number of tasks that can be performed. Attackers can exploit this vulnerability to cause congestion. Malware can also be injected into the platform for resource exhaustion. The entire cloud network can be transformed into a botnet as well. Personal information gathered and stored over the cloud is also susceptible to disclosure. Malicious attackers can also exploit the software bugs or configuration flaws to obtain access to the otherwise protected data and assets.

To manage DoS attacks, techniques such as frequency hopping, channel switching, and utilization of multiple transceivers can be adopted. In addition, a congestion database can be maintained to keep the records of the source of the attack, timing, and frequency. In order to prevent malware-based attacks, an Intrusion Detection System can be deployed and a system integrity check can be performed. To prevent disclosure of personal information, data anonymization techniques can be utilized. In addition, multi-factor protection schemes that can prioritize the user's access actions can also be adopted. To prevent privilege escalation, authentication mechanisms can be embraced to verify the identities of the data- or resource-requesting entities.

6.4.1.3 End-to-End Networking

Pushing application-explicit highlights to the end nodes with a high level of complexity can generate issues in case of unreliable network connections. Besides, bugs or malware present in the vehicular computing system can give rise to various security issues.

To keep away from security risks involved with end-to-end networking, partial control must be distributed to fog nodes for real-time processing. In addition, vehicles can be deployed with advance security capabilities to avoid risks in order to establish an intelligent and self-defending network that can generate alarm in attack situations.

6.4.2 Challenges and Countermeasures Associated with Participating Entities

In this subsection, we discuss the challenges associated with participating entities, along with the countermeasures proposed in the literature.

6.4.2.1 Vehicles

Security issues and countermeasures associated with different technologies involved in the development of CADVs are summarized in Table 6.2.

6.4.2.2 Connection Infrastructure

For establishing communication among vehicles, between the vehicle and the core infrastructure, and between the vehicle and the cloud, various communication methods are used. Different security attacks related to the communication networks include DoS or DDoS attacks, password and key attacks

TABLE 6.2   Vehicle-specific security challenges and existing countermeasures

ENTITY	TECHNOLOGY USED	SECURITY ISSUES/ ATTACKS	SECURITY SOLUTIONS
Vehicles (low-level sensors)	GPS	Rogue signals, Spoofing and Jamming (noisy signals)	Validation mechanisms, Monitoring identification codes and satellite signals, Using time intervals, Threshold-based monitoring of changes in signal, Observing signal strength, Cryptographic mechanisms, Digital signatures
	Inertial Measurement Unit	DoS	Secondary source of measurement through additional sensors
		Interception, Man-in-the-middle (MITM) attack	Encryption mechanisms
		Interference	Encryption mechanisms, Signal monitoring
		Compromising sensors to simulate false data	Deploying control unit to monitor information being transmitted
	Engine control sensor	Modifying packets, Introducing rogue data packets	Cryptographic and authentication mechanisms

(Continued)

TABLE 6.2 (Continued)   Vehicle-specific security challenges and existing countermeasures

ENTITY	TECHNOLOGY USED	SECURITY ISSUES/ ATTACKS	SECURITY SOLUTIONS
	Tire pressure monitor systems	Reverse engineering sniffing Identity tracking	Encryption mechanisms
		Spoofing	Frequency shift keying (FSK) or Amplitude Shift Keying (ASK)
		Manipulation of tire pressure readings and fake warnings	Encryption mechanisms, Frequent updates
	LiDAR	Spoofing, Deceiving, and Jamming	Using different wavelengths, Optical filters, Vehicle-to-Vehicle (V2V) communications, Random probing
	Ultrasonic sensors	Spoofing (random and adaptive) and Jamming	Single sensor-based Physical Shift Authentication (PSA), Multiple sensor consistency check (MSCC)
	Cameras	Blinding camera using high-powered lights	Using camera filters, Increased number of sensors for reliable representation of the environment,
Vehicles (control modules)	Engine Control Unit (ECU)	DoS, Attacker uploading new firmware, Attacking the sensor or exploiting the control module directly, Falsifying sensor data	Cryptographic mechanisms, Frequent updates

(e.g., rainbow table, dictionary, and brute force attacks), network protocol attacks (e.g., spoofing and interception), rogue updates, phishing and ransomware, and so forth [72]. In order to prevent these attacks, some of the already existing methods include adoption of stronger cryptographic mechanisms with large size keys, deploying a distribution model for firmware update, protocol analysis, revocation of privileges, authentication [73], and so on.

Vulnerabilities associated with the large number of ECUs and the underlying software entice attackers to attack CADVs. Attacks associated with physical access can be either direct attacks, such as bus tapping, on-board diagnostic port exploitation, media systems exploitation, removal or replacement of hardware modules, or indirect attacks [74]. Direct attacks can be prevented through access control mechanisms [75], and indirect attacks can be avoided through the appropriate exploitation of the different aspects of the system.

The presence of different sensor units opens ways for disruption by malicious users. Attacks related to close proximity include hijacking attack, Bluetooth device compromise, disorientation, keyless entry, ignition systems exploitation, signal jamming for connected devices (e.g., trivial jamming, periodic, and reactive attack), and so forth. In order to prevent these attacks, signal detection can be done and cryptographic mechanisms-based Bluetooth protocols can be adopted [76].

Wireless communication techniques make CADVs vulnerable to various malicious activities. Remote access vulnerabilities include device compromise, map database poisoning, radio-, cellular-, and Internet-enabled exploits, etc. In order to prevent these attacks, third-party verification and stronger encryption mechanisms along with a plausibility check can be employed.

6.4.2.3 Human Aspects

Although privacy is not considered as an immediate concern, high interconnectivity of the autonomous vehicles makes them vulnerable to hacking that can lead to unauthorized and malicious access to the vehicular data, which in turn can be misused to cause personal damage to the people using it. Thus, ensuring privacy of the people is an important area of concern [77]. Different activities can violate the privacy of drivers, such as tracking a user's location and stalking the driver for theft. These can be prevented through encryption, data anonymization, and trust mechanisms, along with appropriate designing of CADVs and the core infrastructure. An adversary can also exploit the behavioral aspects of user, such as by compromising a non-technical human operator. These can be prevented by educating and training the driver or by monitoring the activities including runtime signal level.

Sherif et al. [78] proposed a scheme that addresses the privacy issues in ridesharing scenarios using a similarity measurement technique on the already encrypted data, enabling users to share rides while maintaining location privacy with other users. Taeihagh et al. [79] discussed the technological risks associated with CADVs and different ways in which cybersecurity and privacy can be achieved.

6.5 ONGOING RESEARCH EFFORTS

MIT AgeLab in a joint effort with Toyota has planned an research initiative, the Collaborative Safety Research Center, for developing and analyzing motion planning and deep learning perceptron-based advances [80]. The venture will concentrate on improving the security and safety of drivers and pedestrians by contemplating the anatomy of accidents. Likewise, the Drive Me project started by Volvo is associated with analyzing the effects of introducing autonomous vehicles to the street transportation framework and collecting statistics related to the traffic flow, energy efficiency, and safety of the vehicles [81]. The Society of Automotive Engineers International is a U.S.-based association engaged in characterizing benchmarks and scientific classification for CADVs [82]. A progressing venture by the University of Michigan (UM) Ford Center for Autonomous Vehicles is focusing on incorporating deep learning techniques with sensor innovation for self-driving cars [83].

Cognitive science along with approaches including Bayesian models and team reasoning concepts are also becoming popular areas of study while designing autonomous driving capabilities [84]. Blockchain technology is also being explored by researchers to establish security features in cloud and edge computing-based autonomous vehicles [85]. Far infrared technology has become an area of research in which a far infrared camera acts as a passive means to sense the signals from the heat radiating objects for detecting these objects [86].

6.6 OPEN RESEARCH CHALLENGES

Although CADVs are envisioned to provide comfort and opportunities by manipulating the interactions of travelers with the transportation systems, there are a plethora of obstacles and research challenges that need to be identified in order to ensure seamless deployment of these systems. These are outlined in the following subsections.

6.6.1 Deployment and Operational Costs

Large-scale adoption of CADVs is limited by the deployment and operational costs. Different components embedded within the vehicles including sensors and navigation technology incur significant costs that are typically not affordable by regular customers [87]. In addition, the operational features like ACC and safety techniques raise the overall operational costs significantly. Thus, cost is an important implementation barrier because of the unaffordability of the underlying technologies involved in the development of CADVs.

6.6.2 Security

Ensuring the security of CADV systems is a constant concern among the manufacturers, policymakers, and drivers. Reliable defense mechanisms need to be developed to prevent the threats and vulnerabilities associated with these systems in order to bring the realization of the corresponding attacks to a different level. Some of the questions that are yet to be answered include updating the CADV software while maintaining the security, switching control between the driver and the underlying automated system in case of a cyber threat, response generation in case of a wide-scale cyber attack, accountability issues, and so on. In addition, processing a large amount of data while at the same time ensuring the secure accessibility and usage of the data is challenging. Security parameters associated with the communication protocols, the core infrastructure, and the vehicles themselves require careful monitoring in order to avoid any disruptions due to malicious entities. However, since a typical CADV system behaves as an access point, it seems practically impossible to make the system completely secure. Moreover, these can be used as a point source to broadcast the attack across other systems. This would pose a great challenge for the hardware and software developers with huge negative consequences. Apart from known vulnerabilities, unknown vulnerabilities also pose security issues and can turn CADVs into a major crime tool [88].

6.6.3 Privacy

Different privacy related concerns associated with CADVs have been raised including the type of data to be collected and stored, data ownership and control, data sharing, entities utilizing the data, location privacy, and so forth. Information associated with source and destination, the route followed by the vehicles, the time and date of travel, and driver's identity require appropriate and adequate safeguards in order to avoid misuse. However, ensuring the safeguards within a heterogeneous working environment consisting of different technologies and involved stakeholders including government organizations, suppliers, agencies involved in surveillance and monitoring, communication service providers, advertisement agencies, policymakers, and designers is an open research challenge. Moreover, the privacy requirements of a self-contained vehicular model and an inter-connected vehicular model are different and require an extra level of effort to understand and fulfill.

6.6.4 Legal and Ethical Aspects

Legal aspects are among the critical challenges and include the technical standards and public policies, along with traffic regulations [89]. There is no appropriate uniform legal framework for testing and using the automated vehicles across the world, which is a hurdle for this technology. According to the Vienna Convention (1968) Article 8, "Every moving vehicle or combination of vehicles shall have a driver," and according to Article 13, "Every driver of a vehicle shall in all circumstances have his vehicle under control," which implies that it does not allow fully automated vehicles in transportation systems [90].

Ethical concerns are also among the most important aspects while implementing CADV systems. CADVs are expected to make correct decisions all the time, including emergencies. For example, there might be a situation in which although the path is clear for the vehicle, a pedestrian suddenly comes in the way. The vehicle is expected to reduce its speed despite the pedestrian breaking the road rules. However, the ultimate responsibility to be imposed in case of an accident is still a dilemma [91]. Thus, there is a need to develop efficient decision-making algorithms to follow the ethical norms.

6.6.5 Validation and Testing

To ensure safety and flawless functioning of CADVs in real-time, there is a demand for a significant effort while designing new concepts and testing systems to evaluate the performance of the vehicles in a simulated environment. Varying components (human participants, underlying software and hardware, and algorithms) and environmental conditions must be considered to validate the functionality of the vehicles [92]. Field Operational Tests are of the utmost importance to analyze and strengthen the safety and reliability of CADVs [90].

6.6.6 Standardization

There is no uniform standard for the underlying infrastructure development, data management, system design, and communication protocols. Different nations across the world are formulating their own standards, and establishing an agreement and harmonizing the agreement is one of the biggest challenges in the field. Because of the different underlying technologies, coordination and standardization of these technologies and security primitives is necessary [93]. However, even if the development of CADVs become standardized and more generic, it would lead to cyber attacks in which hacking a single vehicle can lead to the spread of the attack across other vehicles belonging to a different industry [95].

6.6.7 Other Aspects

The commercial availability of CADVs is accompanied with a high degree of uncertainty. And the promoting factors other than discussed above include regional modeling, operational and connectivity requirements, road infrastructure, transit facilities, policymaking, shared mobility, and so on [95]. Thus, designing next generation autonomous vehicular systems needs to incorporate proper architecture planning, data management, and modeling distributed and parallel computing platforms [3].

6.7 SUMMARY

In spite of the fact that the idea of completely self-governing vehicles may restrict a long effort to go into the market en masse, this innovation is advancing quickly with certain highlights being offered by the vehicle producers in the present models. This innovation is equipped for decreasing mishaps, congestion, improving eco-friendliness, and versatility. In any case, various security issues still remain that are of great concern. Henceforth, it is necessary for engineers and producers to recognize these issues and security attacks that are explicit to this innovation and to address them to standardize the autonomous vehicle industry.

This chapter has featured the key underlying advances and paradigms related to the autonomous vehicular frameworks or CADVs and recognized the potential dangers or attacks related to them alongside the current mitigation methods. Some of the progressing research endeavors and the open research difficulties have additionally been achieved, giving an insight to the future research directions. Some essential changes are required to keep up a high level of security and reliability across clients and the efforts of the policymakers and manufacturers so as to create a powerful core framework and vehicles.

REFERENCES

1. Protiviti. https://www.protiviti.com/US-en/insights/evolution-autonomous-vehicles. Accessed April 2018.
2. Ray, S. (2017, November). Transportation security in the era of autonomous vehicles: Challenges and practice. In *Proceedings of the 36th international conference on computer-aided design* (pp. 1034–1038). IEEE Press.
3. Plathottam, S. J., & Ranganathan, P. (2018, January). Next generation distributed and networked autonomous vehicles. In *2018 10th International Conference on Communication Systems & Networks (COMSNETS)* (pp. 577–582). IEEE.
4. Tewari, A., & Gupta, B. B. (2018). Security, privacy and trust of different layers in Internet-of-Things (IoTs) framework. *Future Generation Computer Systems.* https://doi.org/10.1016/j.future.2018.04.027.
5. Gupta, B. B., & Agrawal, D. P. (Eds.). (2019). *Handbook of research on cloud computing and big data applications in IoT.* Hershey, PA: IGI Global.
6. Adat, V., & Gupta, B. B. (2018). Security in Internet of Things: Issues, challenges, taxonomy, and architecture. *Telecommunication Systems, 67*(3), 423–441.
7. Gupta, B. B. (Ed.). (2018). *Computer and cyber security: Principles, algorithm, applications, and perspectives.* Boca Raton, FL: CRC Press.
8. Gupta, B., Agrawal, D. P., & Yamaguchi, S. (Eds.). (2016). *Handbook of research on modern cryptographic solutions for computer and cyber security.* Hershey, PA: IGI global.
9. McGehee, D. V., Brewer, M., Schwarz, C., & Smith, B. W. (2016). *Review of automated vehicle technology: Policy and implementation implications.* Ames, IA: Iowa Department of Transportation.
10. Dominic, D., Chhawri, S., Eustice, R. M., Ma, D., & Weimerskirch, A. (2016, October). Risk assessment for cooperative automated driving. In *Proceedings of the 2nd ACM workshop on cyber-physical systems security and privacy* (pp. 47–58). ACM.
11. Dey, K. C., Rayamajhi, A., Chowdhury, M., Bhavsar, P., & Martin, J. (2016). Vehicle-to-vehicle (V2V) and vehicle-to-infrastructure (V2I) communication in a heterogeneous wireless network–Performance evaluation. *Transportation Research Part C: Emerging Technologies, 68*, 168–184.
12. Olariu, C., McLoughlin, S., & Thompson, G. (2017, November). Cloud-support for collaborative services in connected cars scenarios. In *Vehicular networking conference (VNC)* (pp. 255–258). IEEE.
13. Rahimian, P., O'Neal, E. E., Zhou, S., Plumert, J. M., & Kearney, J. K. (2018). Harnessing vehicle-to-pedestrian (V2P) communication technology: Sending traffic warnings to texting pedestrians. *Human Factors*, 0018720818781365.

14. Giordani, M., Zanella, A., Higuchi, T., Altintas, O., & Zorzi, M. (2018). Performance study of LTE and mmWave in vehicle-to-network communications. *arXiv preprint arXiv:1805.04271.*
15. Bai, X., & Moradi-Pari, E. (2018). U.S. Patent Application No. 15/942,939.
16. Trepagnier, P. G., Nagel, J. E., Kinney, P. M., Dooner, M. T., Wilson, B. M., Schneider Jr, C. R., & Goeller, K. B. (2011). U.S. Patent No. 8,050,863. Washington, DC: U.S. Patent and Trademark Office.
17. Gong, S., Zhou, A., Wang, J., Li, T., & Peeta, S. (2018). Cooperative adaptive cruise control for a platoon of connected and autonomous vehicles considering dynamic information flow topology. arXiv preprint arXiv:1807.02224.
18. Branson, E. (2018). U.S. Patent Application No. 15/714,750.
19. Gao, H., Cheng, B., Wang, J., Li, K., Zhao, J., & Li, D. (2018). Object classification using CNN-based fusion of vision and LIDAR in autonomous vehicle environment. *IEEE Transactions on Industrial Informatics, 14*(9), 4224–4231.
20. Chesworth, A. A., & Huddleston, J. (2018, January). Precision optical components for lidar systems developed for autonomous vehicles. In *Next-generation optical communication: Components, sub-systems, and systems VII* (Vol. 10561, p. 105610J). International Society for Optics and Photonics.
21. Gleaves, M., Ludlow, P., Christie, S., & Liu, P. (2018, May). Advanced radar for autonomous vehicles and degraded visual environments. In *Society of photo-optical instrumentation engineers (SPIE) conference series* (Vol. 10634).
22. Zofka, M. R., Essinger, M., Fleck, T., Kohlhaas, R., & Zöllner, J. M. (2018, May). The sleepwalker framework: Verification and validation of autonomous vehicles by mixed reality LiDAR stimulation. In *2018 IEEE International Conference on Simulation, Modeling, and Programming for Autonomous Robots (SIMPAR)* (pp. 151–157). IEEE.
23. Cui, Y., & Ge, S. S. (2003). Autonomous vehicle positioning with GPS in urban canyon environments. *IEEE Transactions on Robotics and Automation, 19*(1), 15–25.
24. Liu, Y., Fan, X., Lv, C., Wu, J., Li, L., & Ding, D. (2018). An innovative information fusion method with adaptive Kalman filter for integrated INS/GPS navigation of autonomous vehicles. *Mechanical Systems and Signal Processing, 100,* 605–616.
25. Jun, M., & Markel, A. J. (2017). Infrastructure-Based Sensors Augmenting Efficient Autonomous Vehicle Operations: Preprint (No. NREL/CP-5400-62390). Golder, CO: National Renewable Energy Lab (NREL).
26. Vidhya, D. S., Rebelo, D. P., D'Silva, C. J., Fernandes, L. W., & Costa, C. J. (2016). Obstacle detection using ultrasonic sensors. *International Journal for Innovative Research in Science & Technology, 2*(11), 316–320.
27. Li, S. E., Li, G., Yu, J., Liu, C., Cheng, B., Wang, J., & Li, K. (2018). Kalman filter-based tracking of moving objects using linear ultrasonic sensor array for road vehicles. *Mechanical Systems and Signal Processing, 98,* 173–189.
28. Wang, G., Chong, P. H. J., Seet, B. C., & Zhang, K. (2018, July). The vehicle collision warning method based on the information fusion of GPS/INS and DSRC. In *IOP conference series: Materials science and engineering* (Vol. 394, No. 3, p. 032110). Bristol: IOP Publishing.
29. Elie, L. D., & Rhode, D. S. (2018). U.S. Patent Application No. 15/793,888.

30. Cao, T., Xiang, Z. Y., & Liu, J. L. (2015). Perception in disparity: An efficient navigation framework for autonomous vehicles with stereo cameras. *IEEE Transactions on Intelligent Transportation Systems, 16*(5), 2935–2948.
31. Park, E. S., Yu, C. H., & Choi, J. W. (2015). Development of a lateral control system for autonomous vehicles using data fusion of vision and IMU sensors with field tests. *Journal of Institute of Control, Robotics and Systems, 21*(3), 179–186.
32. Rupp, M. Y., Engelman, G. H., Miller, A. M., Zwicky, T. D., Tellis, L., & Stephenson, R. L. (2015). U.S. Patent No. 9,079,587. Washington, DC: U.S. Patent and Trademark Office.
33. Marin-Plaza, P., Hussein, A., Martin, D., & Escalera, A. D. L. (2018). Global and local path planning study in a ROS-based research platform for autonomous vehicles. *Journal of Advanced Transportation, 2018*, 1–10.
34. Burgard, W., Franke, U., Enzweiler, M., & Trivedi, M. (2016). The mobile revolution-machine intelligence for autonomous vehicles (Dagstuhl Seminar 15462). In *Dagstuhl Reports* (Vol. 5, No. 11). Schloss Dagstuhl-Leibniz-Zentrum fuer Informatik.
35. Seif, H. G., & Hu, X. (2016). Autonomous driving in the iCity—HD maps as a key challenge of the automotive industry. *Engineering, 2*(2), 159–162.
36. Maturana, D., Chou, P. W., Uenoyama, M., & Scherer, S. (2018). Real-time semantic mapping for autonomous off-road navigation. In *Field and Service Robotics* (pp. 335–350). Cham, Switzerland: Springer.
37. Li, B., Yang, L., Xiao, J., Valde, R., Wrenn, M., & Leflar, J. (2018). Collaborative mapping and autonomous parking for multi-story parking garage. *IEEE Transactions on Intelligent Transportation Systems, 19*(5), 1629–1639.
38. Lin, Y. H., Huang, L. C., Chen, S. Y., & Yu, C. M. (2018). The optimal route planning for inspection task of autonomous underwater vehicle composed of MOPSO-based dynamic routing algorithm in currents. *Applied Ocean Research, 75*, 178–192.
39. Durst, P. J., Goodin, C. T., Bethel, C. L., Anderson, D. T., Carruth, D. W., & Lim, H. (2018). A perception-based fuzzy route planning algorithm for autonomous unmanned ground vehicles. *Unmanned Systems.*
40. McAllister, R., Gal, Y., Kendall, A., Van Der Wilk, M., Shah, A., Cipolla, R., & Weller, A. V. (2017, August). Concrete problems for autonomous vehicle safety: Advantages of Bayesian deep learning. *International Joint Conferences on Artificial Intelligence.*
41. Wuthishuwong, C., Traechtler, A., & Bruns, T. (2015). Safe trajectory planning for autonomous intersection management by using vehicle to infrastructure communication. *EURASIP Journal on Wireless Communications and Networking, 2015*(1), 33.
42. González, D., Pérez, J., Milanés, V., & Nashashibi, F. (2016). A review of motion planning techniques for automated vehicles. *IEEE Transactions on Intelligent Transportation Systems, 17*(4), 1135–1145.
43. Zhang, C., Hu, J., Qiu, J., Yang, W., Sun, H., & Chen, Q. (2018). A novel fuzzy observer-based steering control approach for path tracking in autonomous vehicles. *IEEE Transactions on Fuzzy Systems, 27*(2), 278–290.
44. Schambers, A., Eavis-O'Quinn, M., Roberge, V., & Tarbouchi, M. (2018, April). Route planning for electric vehicle efficiency using the Bellman-Ford algorithm on an embedded GPU. In *2018 4th International Conference on Optimization and Applications (ICOA)* (pp. 1–6). IEEE.

45. Maurer, M., Gerdes, J. C., Lenz, B., & Winner, H. (2016). *Autonomous driving*. Berlin, Germany: Springer.
46. Greenblatt, J. B., & Saxena, S. (2015). Autonomous taxis could greatly reduce greenhouse-gas emissions of US light-duty vehicles. *Nature Climate Change*, 5(9), 860.
47. Statista. https://www.statista.com/statistics/428692/projected-size-of-global-autonomous-vehicle-market-by-vehicle-type/. Accessed August 2018.
48. Litman, T. (2017). *Autonomous vehicle implementation predictions*. Victoria, Canada: Victoria Transport Policy Institute.
49. Techemergence. https://www.techemergence.com/self-driving-car-timeline-themselves-top-11-automakers/. Accessed August 2018.
50. Gartner Survey Reveals 55 Percent of Respondents Will Not Ride in a Fully Autonomous Vehicle. https://www.gartner.com/newsroom/id/3790963. Accessed November 2017.
51. Zhang, X., Gao, H., Guo, M., Li, G., Liu, Y., & Li, D. (2016). A study on key technologies of unmanned driving. *CAAI Transactions on Intelligence Technology*, 1(1), 4–13.
52. Bertozzi, M., Broggi, A., Cellario, M., Fascioli, A., Lombardi, P., & Porta, M. (2002). Artificial vision in road vehicles. *Proceedings of the IEEE*, 90(7), 1258–1271.
53. Chen, Y., Peng, H., & Grizzle, J. (2018). Obstacle avoidance for low-speed autonomous vehicles with barrier function. *IEEE Transactions on Control Systems Technology*, 26(1), 194–206.
54. Guerrero-Ibanez, J. A., Zeadally, S., & Contreras-Castillo, J. (2015). Integration challenges of intelligent transportation systems with connected vehicle, cloud computing, and Internet of Things technologies. *IEEE Wireless Communications*, 22(6), 122–128.
55. Yan, G., Wen, D., Olariu, S., & Weigle, M. C. (2013). Security challenges in vehicular cloud computing. *IEEE Transactions on Intelligent Transportation Systems*, 14(1), 284–294.
56. Gerla, M., Lee, E. K., Pau, G., & Lee, U. (2014, March). Internet of vehicles: From intelligent grid to autonomous cars and vehicular clouds. In *Internet of Things (WF-IoT), 2014 IEEE world forum on* (pp. 241–246). IEEE.
57. Muller, U., Ben, J., Cosatto, E., Flepp, B., & Cun, Y. L. (2006). Off-road obstacle avoidance through end-to-end learning. In *Advances in neural information processing systems* (pp. 739–746).
58. Xu, H., Gao, Y., Yu, F., & Darrell, T. (2017). End-to-end learning of driving models from large-scale video datasets. arXiv preprint.
59. Bojarski, M., Del Testa, D., Dworakowski, D., Firner, B., Flepp, B., Goyal, P., & Zhang, X. (2016). End to end learning for self-driving cars. arXiv preprint arXiv:1604.07316.
60. Karnouskos, S., & Kerschbaum, F. (2018). Privacy and integrity considerations in hyperconnected autonomous vehicles. *Proceedings of the IEEE*, 106(1), 160–170.
61. Amoozadeh, M., Raghuramu, A., Chuah, C. N., Ghosal, D., Zhang, H. M., Rowe, J., & Levitt, K. (2015). Security vulnerabilities of connected vehicle streams and their impact on cooperative driving. *IEEE Communications Magazine*, 53(6), 126–132.

62. Thing, V. L., & Wu, J. (2016, December). Autonomous vehicle security: A taxonomy of attacks and defences. In *2016 IEEE International Conference on Internet of Things (iThings) and IEEE green computing and communications (GreenCom) and IEEE cyber, physical and social computing (CPSCom) and IEEE smart data (SmartData)* (pp. 164–170). IEEE.

63. Petit, J., & Shladover, S. E. (2015). Potential cyberattacks on automated vehicles. *IEEE Transactions on Intelligent Transportation Systems, 16*(2), 546–556.

64. Amodei, D., Olah, C., Steinhardt, J., Christiano, P., Schulman, J., & Mané, D. (2016). Concrete problems in AI safety. arXiv preprint arXiv:1606.06565.

65. Rodrigues, M., McGordon, A., Gest, G., & Marco, J. (2017, April). Developing and testing of control software framework for autonomous ground vehicle. In *2017 IEEE International Conference on Autonomous Robot Systems and Competitions (ICARSC)* (pp. 4–10). IEEE.

66. Lu, J., Sibai, H., Fabry, E., & Forsyth, D. (2017). No need to worry about adversarial examples in object detection in autonomous vehicles. arXiv preprint arXiv:1707.03501.

67. George, N., & Thomas, J. (2018, August). Authenticating communication of autonomous vehicles with artificial intelligence. In *IOP Conference Series: Materials Science and Engineering* (Vol. 396, No. 1, p. 012017). Bristol: IOP Publishing.

68. Siau, K., & Wang, W. (2018). Building trust in artificial intelligence, machine learning, and robotics. *Cutter Business Technology Journal, 31*(2), 47–53.

69. Ali Alheeti, K. M., & McDonald-Maier, K. (2018). Intelligent intrusion detection in external communication systems for autonomous vehicles. *Systems Science & Control Engineering, 6*(1), 48–56.

70. Lee, E., Lee, E. K., Gerla, M., & Oh, S. Y. (2014). Vehicular cloud networking: Architecture and design principles. *IEEE Communications Magazine, 52*(2), 148–155.

71. Joy, J., Rabsatt, V., & Gerla, M. (2018). Internet of Vehicles: Enabling safe, secure, and private vehicular crowdsourcing. *Internet Technology Letters, 1*(1), e16.

72. Hamida, E. B., Noura, H., & Znaidi, W. (2015). Security of cooperative intelligent transport systems: Standards, threats analysis and cryptographic countermeasures. *Electronics, 4*(3), 380–423.

73. Lohachab, A. (2018). Using quantum key distribution and ECC for secure inter-device authentication and communication in IoT infrastructure. In *Proceedings of 3rd International Conference on Internet of Things and Connected Technologies (ICIoTCT)* (pp. 26–27).

74. Wyglinski, A. M., Huang, X., Padir, T., Lai, L., Eisenbarth, T. R., & Venkatasubramanian, K. (2013). Security of autonomous systems employing embedded computing and sensors. *IEEE Micro, 33*(1), 80–86.

75. Gupta, B. B., & Quamara, M. (2018). An identity based access control and mutual authentication framework for distributed cloud computing services in IoT environment using smart cards. *Procedia Computer Science, 132*, 189–197.

76. Cheah, M., Shaikh, S. A., Haas, O., & Ruddle, A. (2017). Towards a systematic security evaluation of the automotive Bluetooth interface. *Vehicular Communications, 9*, 8–18.

77. Glancy, D. J. (2012). Privacy in autonomous vehicles. *Santa Clara Law Review*, *52*, 1171.

78. Sherif, A. B., Rabieh, K., Mahmoud, M. M., & Liang, X. (2017). Privacy-preserving ride sharing scheme for autonomous vehicles in big data era. *IEEE Internet of Things Journal*, *4*(2), 611–618.

79. Taeihagh, A., & Lim, H. S. M. (2018). Governing autonomous vehicles: Emerging responses for safety, liability, privacy, cybersecurity, and industry risks. *Transport Reviews*, 1–26.

80. CSRC 2017 Report. http://corporatenews.pressroom.toyota.com/releases/csrc+2017+report.htm. Accessed December 2017.

81. Victor, T., Rothoff, M., Coelingh, E., Ödblom, A., & Burgdorf, K. (2017). When autonomous vehicles are introduced on a larger scale in the road transport system: The Drive Me project. In *Automated Driving* (pp. 541–546). Cham: Springer International Publishing.

82. Automated Driving – SAE International. https://www.smmt.co.uk/wp-content/uploads/sites/2/automated_driving.pdf. Accessed December 2017.

83. Johnson-Roberson, M., Barto, C., Mehta, R., Sridhar, S. N., Rosaen, K., & Vasudevan, R. (2017, May). Driving in the matrix: Can virtual worlds replace human-generatedannotations for real world tasks? In *2017 IEEE International Conference on Robotics and Automation (ICRA)* (pp. 746–753). IEEE.

84. Chater, N., Misyak, J., Watson, D., Griffiths, N., & Mouzakitis, A. (2018). Negotiating the traffic: Can cognitive science help make autonomous vehicles a reality? *Trends in Cognitive Sciences*, *22*(2), 93–95.

85. Liu, H., Zhang, Y., & Yang, T. (2018). Blockchain-enabled security in electric vehicles cloud and edge computing. *IEEE Network*, *32*(3), 78–83.

86. Kim, T., & Kim, S. (2018). Pedestrian detection at night time in FIR domain: Comprehensive study about temperature and brightness and new benchmark. *Pattern Recognition*, *79*, 44–54.

87. Daziano, R. A., Sarrias, M., & Leard, B. (2017). Are consumers willing to pay to let cars drive for them? Analyzing response to autonomous vehicles. *Transportation Research Part C: Emerging Technologies*, *78*, 150–164.

88. Takefuji, Y. (2018). Connected vehicle security vulnerabilities [commentary]. *IEEE Technology and Society Magazine*, *37*(1), 15–18.

89. Barabás, I., Todoruţ, A., Cordoş, N., & Molea, A. (2017, October). Current challenges in autonomous driving. In *IOP Conference Series: Materials Science and Engineering* (Vol. 252, No. 1, p. 012096). Bristol: IOP Publishing.

90. Dokic, J., Müller, B., & Meyer, G. (2015). European roadmap smart systems for automated driving. *European Technology Platform on Smart Systems Integration*, *2015*, 1–39.

91. Hevelke, A., & Nida-Rümelin, J. (2015). Responsibility for crashes of autonomous vehicles: An ethical analysis. *Science and Engineering Ethics*, *21*(3), 619–630.

92. Vishnukumar, H. J., Butting, B., Müller, C., & Sax, E. (2017, September). Machine learning and deep neural network—Artificial intelligence core for lab and real-world test and validation for ADAS and autonomous vehicles: AI for efficient and quality test and validation. In *Intelligent systems conference (IntelliSys), 2017* (pp. 714–721). IEEE.

93. Schoitsch, E., Schmittner, C., Ma, Z., & Gruber, T. (2016). The need for safety and cyber-security co-engineering and standardization for highly automated automotive vehicles. In *Advanced microsystems for automotive applications 2015* (pp. 251–261). Cham, Switzerland: Springer.
94. University of Michigan. Assessing risk: Identifying and analyzing cybersecurity threats to automated vehicles. https://www.clickondetroit.com/all-about-ann-arbor/2018/01/04/university-of-michigans-mcity-releases-threat-identifying-tool-for-automated-vehicles/. Accessed July 2018.
95. Fagnant, D. J., & Kockelman, K. (2015). Preparing a nation for autonomous vehicles: Opportunities, barriers and policy recommendations. *Transportation Research Part A: Policy and Practice, 77,* 167–181.

Index

Note: Page numbers in italic and bold refer to figures and tables, respectively.